NUDGED

Moved by God

Uplifting True Stories of Faith

SUSAN BROWNELL

DISCLAIMER: This book is intended to offer inspirational support and
encouragement. It is not intended to offer medical advice or take the place
of advice or treatment from trained medical professionals. If you have health
questions or concerns about yourself or a loved one, you should seek professional
medical care. The publisher and author disclaim all liability that may be the
result of the use of or misuse of any medical or non-medical information
contained within this book.

Published by: S B Leeder Publishing, Sparta, Wisconsin 54656
www.SusanBrownell.com
info@SusanBrownell.com

Cover and interior images used under license from Shutterstock:
Khabarushka/Shutterstock.com (https://shutterstock.com)
MacroVector/Shutterstock.com (https://shutterstock.com)
Lavendertime/Shutterstock.com (https://shutterstock.com)
Editing by Word-2-Kindle
Cover and interior design by Word-2-Kindle

ISBN 978-1-940826-05-9 (Paperback)
ISBN 978-1-940826-14-1 (Ebook)

Library of Congress Control Number: 2024924837

Since you are my rock and my fortress,
for the sake of your name lead and guide me.

Psalm 31:3 NIV

CONTENTS

INTRODUCTION

"But how do you know?" she said as she looked me in the eye. It was a good question. A friend and I had been discussing some personal issues we both had been experiencing. I mentioned to her that I had been at a loss for what to do and felt quite overwhelmed and stressed. I went on to tell her that after much prayerful consideration and time spent reading the Bible, I felt I had received guidance on how to handle the problem.

Her question was, "How do we recognize messages from God that are meant to guide us?" It was a fair question. It was one I felt a bit challenged to answer.

What she really wanted to know was: How does God give us the answers we are looking for? How do we know when he wants us to do something? How does he speak to our heart? How does God move us?"

I have experienced many instances of feeling God's guiding hand in my life. It was something I felt confident of, yet putting it into words to explain it was difficult. It seemed a bit off to say, "I just know, that's all," even though many times that is what I had felt. I knew I owed her a better answer than that. How can you know something yet struggle to put it into words? Things of faith are sometimes like that. You can know something in your heart and grasp it mentally, but explaining it to another person might be very challenging.

We sometimes forget that God will lead you and guide you. He will nudge you in the right direction. Will you recognize it when he does so?

You are about to read some inspiring true stories. This book isn't about the wonderful people who shared their stories with me. It's about God. You'll read about some things that happened to me. This book isn't about me either. It's about God.

It's about how he intervenes in people's lives. It's about how he reaches us, teaches us, moves us, prompts us, and touches us deep within our heart. It's about how he gets us to react and do things. It's about nudges from God. It's about being aware, watching, and listening. It's about being in God's Word and in prayer. It's about having a real relationship with him. It's about recognizing what he has done in our lives and responding to that. It's about following him. It's about doing the Lord's work on this earth. But mostly, it's about knowing him better.

I used to think I had a personal relationship with God. I didn't think of it in terms of a relationship as much as I thought of it in terms of believing in God and having faith in God. I used to think that. But God was at work on me, and over time, he showed me that although I had faith and believed, I needed to dig deeper and build that relationship with him. I needed to take it to another level. Especially if I wanted any kind of peace in my life. I needed to work on that relationship. And that changed everything.

God doesn't always come to us in ways that we expect. He doesn't conform to our logic. Life as a Christian means we recognize that his ways are not like our ways. Sometimes, we may think God has abandoned us, when in reality, he was with us all along. We may have failed to recognize his presence in our life. He is far bigger than our earthly ways of thinking. His ways cannot be contained within our simple-minded expectations. Yes, he sometimes speaks to us through dramatic events. But often, he speaks to us through simple, everyday events. He reaches us when we are doing everyday tasks. He touches us as we live our everyday lives. He comes to us in a Bible verse, in a song, through a stranger, a friend, or a struggle. He touches our hearts in times of grief, times of need, and in happy times, as well. And through those events, people, circumstances, Bible verses, and sermons, he moves us. How does he move us? He prompts us to take action, make changes in our lives, follow him, grow our faith, do a task, help others, spread his good news, and so much more. In this book, you will read of some dramatic and even a few miraculous nudges. You will also read of many simple, everyday nudges.

God doesn't always display a big glaring advertisement of what he has done in our lives. You won't find any rolling credits at the end of a situation, such as "This divine intervention is brought to you by God" or "This miracle is sponsored by God, the same guy who parted the Red Sea". But…being in God's Word and being a lifelong learner of his will help you to recognize his hand in your life. Being able to recognize those things is such a blessing and encouragement in life!

God has missions for us. He has plans. We don't always know what specific things we are to be doing without a little help from him. God knows that we are all at different points in our journey of faith. He meets us where we are. And then…he gives us a nudge. He nudges us to continue to move along in that journey of faith. Sometimes, we need that, much like a toddler who needs to be coaxed to step out into the big, unknown world.

We all get nudges from God. The question is, do we recognize our nudges as being from God? Are we aware of how God speaks to us? God's nudges take many forms. He may be trying to get us to do something. He may be trying to get us to draw closer to Him. He might be trying to change our hearts.

You see, sometimes it's a little scary to let our guard down and really build a relationship with God—to let him into our innermost thoughts and cares. To depend on him for everything. It makes us feel vulnerable. Sometimes, it's a little scary to acknowledge that something that has happened in our life was God at work. But then, after you acknowledge it and open yourself up to his presence and involvement in your life, you never want to go back. You never want to go back to that weak, lost, and spiritually immature person you used to be. You never want to go back to feeling like you have to be in control. You never want to go back to that place of uncertainty and fear. You never want to go back. Why? Because you have been nudged. Nudged by God.

What Is A Nudge From God?

God's presence in our lives can sometimes go unnoticed by us. It makes one wonder what we may have missed along our earthly journey. With all our Heavenly Father has done for us, it would be sad if we failed to take notice of his hand in our life and thank him.

The deeper relationship we have with God, the more aware we are of his presence in our lives. God is here for us day-to-day, minute-to-minute. He wants us to share our deepest concerns. He wants us to worship and praise him. He wants us to come to him with hearts full of thanksgiving. He wants us to look to him first, not after we have tried to fix things ourselves or failed to get the help we need elsewhere. He doesn't want us to come to him as a last resort. He wants to be first in our lives. He wants a real relationship with us. He told us so in Jeremiah.

You will seek me and find me
when you search for me with all your heart.

Jeremiah 29:13

How does this relationship develop? Think about how our earthly relationships develop. It takes interaction to create and grow a relationship. It takes spending time together. It takes conversations. Deep conversations from the heart. As we spiritually mature, we find we have a deeper relationship with God. We pray and talk to him throughout our day. This goes hand in hand with a stronger faith and trust in him. It can also increase our awareness of how present he is in our lives. Ongoing Bible study and prayer are important components to developing that relationship.

Have you ever stared into space on a crisp fall evening and thought how insignificant we appear to be in the universe? Have you stopped to consider that beyond our galaxy and solar system, space just seems to go on and on? It certainly makes us think about how much God has created. It makes us think about all the people living on Earth today…an estimated eight billion. It can feel like we have a rather insignificant place in all of God's creation. We know that we are all different. We all have many things going on in our lives, and yet, he knows each of us. He knows of our struggles. He understands our fears. Each of us is special to him.

It is difficult to comprehend how he knows each of us that well and wants a personal relationship with each of us. We are truly blessed!

So, back to my friend's question. How do you know? How do you recognize messages from God that are meant to guide us? How does he speak to our hearts? How does he lead and guide us to do what he wants us to do? How does he give us the answers we are looking for? How does God move us?

Having a relationship with God helps open the door to being able to recognize his messages to us. How does God speak to our hearts with messages of encouragement or lead us to things that he wants us to do? He uses several ways. I like to call them "nudges." His Word, which we find in the Bible, may nudge us to take notice. He's trying to get his message through to us so that we can respond to it.

What is a nudge from God? It's a tug on our hearts. It's a prompt from God. It's a cue. It may be our conscience reminding us of something. We may be moved by a Bible verse, a sermon, or a comment from someone. It's a prompting from his Word, from the Holy Spirit. It's a stirring within us that we need to make a change, take action, or do something. It's a stirring that won't leave us alone. It is a stirring that is not contrary to the word of God.

A nudge from God moves us. It causes us to have a change of heart, an improved attitude. It moves us to take action or change our ways. It is God guiding us along a path. A path that we may not always understand. We may resist. We may struggle. And yes, we may go willingly.

A nudge from God isn't necessarily a miracle, although it could be. A nudge from God doesn't have to be dramatic, although it might be. A nudge from God is most often an everyday thing that he uses to touch us, to move us, to get our attention, and to send us to do what he would have us do. He may make us notice something that has happened in our lives or the lives of others. A nudge from God can sometimes be a reminder. Nudges don't have to be extraordinary, but they can be. Nudges are often ordinary. Are your eyes open to recognizing the nudges in your life?

A nudge from God is God knocking on the door of our hearts, letting us know that he is near...that he truly wants us and is claiming us to be his own. Sometimes, a nudge from God is saying, "Is anybody home? Are you listening? You belong to me, but do you want me in your life?" Sometimes, a nudge from God is saying, "May I have your attention, please? You are living recklessly. Some changes need to be made." At other times, a nudge from God says, "I love you. I care for you. I am here for you. There is nothing that you have done that I won't forgive you for if you will only repent and ask for my forgiveness. I have already done the hard work. I sent my Son to die for you. Because of his great love and sacrifice, I have given you the gift of eternal life. Will you follow me?" There are also those times when a nudge from God may be saying, "I know life is difficult. I know you are hurting. Just trust me. I have a plan. You are going to be okay. I will see to it."

God moves us through his Word found in the Bible, through sermons in church, Bible classes, and prayer. He can also move us through having a personal relationship with Jesus and through the power of the Holy Spirit. He can touch us through our interaction with other Christians and even through some unique and special circumstances. You will see many examples of this throughout this book.

How Do We Recognize God's Nudges?

It is God working in our hearts that reveals these nudges. The closer relationship we have with him, the easier it is to recognize these nudges for what they are.

God guides us subtly through the Holy Spirit. But how? When he speaks to us, it is not with audible words. Among other ways, he uses our conscience to guide us.

Our conscience may weigh heavily on us. We may feel a need or a responsibility to do something, change something in our lives, or help someone. We may get this impression repeatedly. That is God giving you a little nudge. We respond according to God's Word and Christian principles.

Romans 9:1 in the NIV version of the Bible says, "I speak the truth in Christ—I am not lying, *my conscience confirms it through the Holy Spirit*—"The Amplified Classic version of the Bible puts it this way: "I am speaking the truth in Christ. I am not lying; *my conscience [enlightened and prompted] by the Holy Spirit* bearing witness with me."

How can this be? How can the Holy Spirit enlighten and prompt us? Because he lives on the inside of us! In 2 Timothy 1:14, the NIV version of the Bible, we read: "Guard the good deposit that was entrusted to you—guard it with the help of **the Holy Spirit who lives in us**."

Sometimes we ask God for nudges when we are looking for his guidance. Often, God just sends us the nudges. Remember, he has plans for us and he is nudging us along towards executing those plans.

God leads and guides us with his nudges to keep us safe. He knows we need his help. He knows we need a shepherd to look after us. He knows we need a shepherd to follow. That shepherd is Jesus Christ. He knows we don't always stay with his flock. We are easily distracted. We might get lost. We are easily lured to wander off in the wrong direction. On occasion, we might even resist his gentle guidance.

Our life situations can vary in seriousness and intensity. Sometimes it doesn't take much for us to recognize our need for God's guidance and respond to his nudge. At other times, we may find ourselves in some more serious situations before we recognize and respond to his nudge.

Often, the nudges are subtle. They might be easily missed if we aren't paying attention. In our quiet moments of reflection, Bible readings, and prayer, we might hear his gentle call. Not an audible voice, but a still, small voice speaking to our heart. A gentle pull. A knowing. A prompt. A cue.

> *"Oh Lord, I see you have a plan for me. Thank you for helping me to see it. Help me to follow through and do as you would have me do."*

Sometimes God wants to ensure he gets our attention and makes the nudge a little stronger. If we are really listening to him, we should pick up on that. It makes me think of someone feeling as though he doesn't have your full attention, but wanting it, so he taps you on the shoulder. Not that God will physically tap you on the shoulder, but this nudge may be a bit more obvious. It should be getting our attention by now.

> *"Dear Lord, I guess I wasn't paying attention. I guess I needed a bit of an eye-opener to see what you wanted me to do all along. Thanks for looking after me. I'm on it, Lord."*

And then, there are those of us who need some extra help because we have been ignoring or oblivious to God's gentle nudges. There are times when he really wants your attention. He wants to wake us up. We might be distracted. We might be zoned out and we are not picking up on his nudges. I hope that God has a sense of humor because when I am struggling with decisions, I have sometimes asked God to throw a brick at me. When I say that, it is because I know that I need God to get me back on track. I might need to snap out of it. Perhaps I need to change my ways. I might be at a loss as to what to do.

> *"I don't always get it, Lord. Please make it very obvious what you want me to do. I don't mind if you throw a brick at me if that's what it takes to get through to me. I need your guidance."*

On rare occasions, we are so tuned in to ourselves, our difficult situation, or our desires that we are oblivious to God's nudges. We may be struggling. God has already tried many ways to get our attention, but we just aren't recognizing it or responding. Things might be spiraling out of control in our lives, and we are in desperate need of help. God may have something he wants us to do, and we have resisted him every step of the way. We might be living a reckless lifestyle. Our life might be in danger. We may have wandered too far from our faith.

On those rare occasions, we might experience a cliffhanger moment in our life. We are hanging by a thin, frayed rope from that cliff. Cliffhangers are scary. God isn't being mean. We may not have been responsive to his prior nudges for various reasons. Life circumstances might cloud our vision and obscure our awareness. Sometimes, we don't pay attention or respond until things have become very serious. Then, we might be more receptive to God's nudge. Remember, he has plans for us.

At times, we shut God out and ignore the prior nudges. We don't always want God to remind us that there's something we need to deal with, and ignoring him won't make it go away. If you let him, he will help you with it. Whatever you do, don't let go of your lifeline to God while hanging from that cliff!

> *"Okay, you've got my attention now, Lord. I know this is serious. I'm sorry I haven't been more responsive to you. You have been trying to get my attention and help me, and in my sinful nature, I have not been listening. I foolishly thought I was in charge. Things have been spiraling out of control. There's uncertainty in my life. I can't handle this on my own. Please help me figure this out. I don't want to go over the cliff."*

At times, there may be something we want to do, but he doesn't want us to do. He may be guiding us.

What if you just aren't sure? Check to see if anything about this nudge is contrary to the Word of God. That is the litmus test. God gave us a conscience for a reason. When in doubt, go to the Bible, pray, talk to the pastor, or ask another Christian for guidance. Again, ask God to make it very clear to you. Then watch, wait, and listen. This takes time and patience.

Don't Judge the Nudge!

When you recognize your nudge, you will more than likely have a reaction to it.

Oh, thank you, Lord! I am so pleased.

Oh, I'm not so sure I want to do THAT, Lord. That is going to take me out of my comfort zone. Could you send me another nudge, please?

Well, how about later, Lord? Could I do that at another time?

If you are confident that this nudge is from God, you can take action and do what you must do with it. Sometimes we don't want to do what we are nudged to do. If the nudge is truly from God, we must remember: Don't judge the nudge! God is in control, not us. Sometimes we have trouble accepting that. There may be something he wants us to do. He may be calling us. We shouldn't ignore those calls.

⁓

For God's gifts and his call are irrevocable.

Romans 11:29 NIV

⁓

SUSAN BROWNELL

Recognizing the Nudge

Writing this book is the result of a nudge from God. I had conversation after conversation with Christians who weren't sure how to recognize when God was speaking to their hearts and where he was leading them. He put it in my heart that I should write this book. Nudged! I resisted at first.

Oh Lord, I would love to write a book for you, but I don't know...I am just a normal person. Are you really sure you want ME to do this? Surely, there are others out there who could do a better job than me. But I would like to do it. I will think about it, Lord.

Oh, don't misunderstand. I really wanted to write this book—eventually. I just wasn't sure now was the right time. I already had another book I was working on. I wanted to finish it first. I had some things going on with my health. I didn't have much energy. I wasn't sure I was the best equipped to do the job. But God had other plans. He kept reminding me about this book. Nudged again!

He kept involving me in conversations with people who didn't understand how he nudges us in our lives. They knew I had experienced nudges. I am just an everyday Christian trying to do what God wants me to do. In my eyes, I am nobody special. But I know that in God's eyes, we are all special. I believe God nudges all of his people. I had told some people about some rather significant nudges I had gotten in the past few years. God's nudges guided me through some turbulent and difficult times. God's nudges had grown my faith and trust in him. People were curious. They were asking questions. They wanted answers. More nudges!

How many more, I wondered? With all the questions I was getting asked from my own circle of acquaintances, how many others

xviii

out there were wondering the same thing? Could it be there really was a need for this book? Could it be I really was supposed to write it? This was going to require some prayer and some thoughtfulness.

❧

Devote yourselves to prayer,
Being watchful and thankful.

Colossians 4:2 NIV

❧

Analyzing the Nudge

As I thought about writing this book, I had one big question. Where would I get all the material? Oh, sure, I had some stories to share. But I needed more. I didn't feel I had enough for a book. If I put out a call for stories, would people be willing to share their stories? I knew some people who had stories, but they were personal stories. Often, people are reluctant to share their personal stories. What if I put out a call for stories to write this book and people didn't respond? What if I didn't get enough stories to fill a book? Would I look like a fool? Should I be mentioning this to anyone when I don't have enough stories yet to fill a book?

God reminded me of my age and my health. I knew there were no guarantees of how long he would leave me here on this earth to do this work for him. He reminded me that working on the computer for long periods of time was getting to be more challenging. Maybe I should think and pray about this some more.

The Bible tells us of many people who felt unworthy of doing tasks God set before them. I couldn't help but think about Moses.

But Moses said to God, "Who am I
that I should go to Pharaoh and bring the Israelites out
of Egypt?" And God said, "I will be with you..."

Exodus 3:11-12 NIV

Now what I was being nudged to do certainly didn't compare to the mighty task that was set before Moses. But what did compare was an important point in this matter. God told Moses he wouldn't be alone, and I knew that I wouldn't be alone. I couldn't possibly do this alone. I knew that God would be with me.

He helped me see there were more people than I imagined who were puzzled by his process of nudging people. He kept nudging me, prodding me, and finally, he gave me a push to make this book the first priority. He's persistent like that. And that's fine with me. What a blessing that he doesn't give up on us!

Commit to the Lord whatever you do,
and he will establish your plans.

Proverbs 16:3 NIV

Responding to the Nudge

God was leading me with his nudge. How would I respond?

If that's your next assignment for me, Lord, let's do it! I'll adjust my plans accordingly. It is you, Lord, who has the final say in what is scheduled in my daily planner, not me. Who am I to say no to God? Who am I to say, "I'd rather do it later?" Who am I to say, "This isn't the best time for me, Lord." Who am I to say, "This is going to be hard, Lord. Where will I get all the material? Will people be willing to share their stories?" I get it, Lord. I know that you want me to do this, so let's get started right now!

Oh, and Lord, I am so honored to get to do this for you. I am humbled by this nudge. Please guide me. Please touch people's hearts to share the stories you want shared with others. Please give me the strength and endurance to do this project, for I can't do it without you. Please lead me down the path you want me to go with this book. Please let this work be pleasing in your sight. Please let this work be a blessing to others. Your humble servant thanks you, Lord, for giving me this nudge to serve you. Thank you for giving me the ability and the opportunity to do this for you. I put my trust in you. In Jesus's name. Amen.

Whatever you do, work at it with all your heart,
as working for the Lord, not for human masters.

Colossians 3:23 NIV

Not that we are competent in ourselves
to claim anything for ourselves,
but our competence comes from God.

2 Cor 3:5 NIV

Once again, scriptures were helping to guide me. God was reminding me that he equips us for the work he gives us to do. I was very thankful for those reminders.

And God is able to bless you abundantly,
so that in all things at all times,
having all that you need,
you will abound in every good work.

2 Cor 9:8 NIV

And so it began…early mornings and late nights spent at the keyboard. An excitement to get up in the morning and start writing, but only after some time spent on devotions and prayer. I tried to begin each writing session with a prayer for guidance on what to write that particular day. There was a standard to meet. After all, this work was for the Lord. It had to be to a high standard. It had to be real and true. It had to be pleasing to the Lord. It had to touch souls, mend hearts, and make people ponder on these things. There was a sense of urgency, responsibility, excitement, enthusiasm, and adventure all rolled together.

The urgency was to do the Lord's work. The responsibility was to get it right. The excitement was an enthusiasm to accomplish this work and do so in a way that was God-pleasing and effective. The adventure was to know that I would soon be hearing about people's faith-based experiences that I had never heard before. Experiences that would touch me and grow my faith and knowledge even further. Experiences that would challenge me, stretch me, and push me to learn and understand even more about how God works in our lives. Finally, there was a realization. I get to write a book about what the Lord has done in people's lives. Not that I have to, but I get to!

I still wasn't completely sure how I was going to handle this project. But I knew that God knew, and I had to trust that he would lead me in the right direction. I needed to "wait for the Lord". He would reveal his plans to me as he deemed necessary. It was a step out of faith and trust on my part. As long as I kept my focus on serving God through this project, I knew he would guide me. I thought about a favorite inspirational quote.

When I stand before God at the end of my life,
I would hope that I would not have a single bit of talent left,
and could say, 'I used everything you gave me'.

~ Erma Bombeck ~

That was me. I wanted to use everything he gave me. And so the adventure began.

Prepare to be Nudged by God

We live in an age with an extreme amount of distractions. People live life multi-tasking on their phones, playing video games, and watching TV. They are bombarded with negativity, gossip, slander, and judgment through social media and computers. There's just too much "noise" in the world. The rush of activity of day-to-day living takes up most of our waking hours, leaving little time for anything else.

It is amazing to think of how many years ago the scripture was written. It was a different age. There were no cell phones, no computers, no TVs, and no video games. Yet, in His omniscience, God knew what his people needed, even in this age. God's inspired Word remains relevant today and provides the timeless guidance so badly needed for those living in this noisy world. The Bible says, "**Be still** and know that I am God." How can we connect with God if we are constantly bombarded with this worldly noise all of our waking hours? It is just not conducive to building and maintaining a relationship with him.

⁓

He says, "Be still and know that I am God…"

Psalm 46:10 NIV

⁓

We might miss some of God's messages and nudges if we are distracted and not listening. We need to open up some time in our day to listen and to be still. We need to release our anxieties and fears to God and accept the peace he freely gives.

We speak to God in prayer. We praise him. We thank him. We confess our sins. He listens. We ask for guidance, comfort, blessings, or resolution to a problem. Then we wait. He may respond to us through various methods. He may make us wait. Whether he answers right away or not, we know he hears our prayers, and he will respond in his own way and on his timetable. In doing so, he teaches us trust, patience, and humility. He nudges us to love, to help others, and to serve him. He nudges us to trust him for help with our problems. Just as we wait for God's response to our prayers, he waits for our response to his nudges.

First Nudges

Nudges aren't just for adults. Even though it impacted me as a child, it wasn't until I grew older that I realized more fully the impact of this nudge at such a young age. The following story is the first nudge I can remember as a child.

CHAPTER 1

Do Cornmeal Pancakes Taste Anything Like Manna?

For some reason, I couldn't get to sleep. Usually, I fell asleep right away. I tossed and turned. The year was 1957. I was nine years old and in fourth grade. I was the oldest of the children and there were babies in the house. Things weren't easy during those years. We made do with what we had.

As I lay awake, soft voices drifted up the stairway and through the heat register to my bedroom. "Marvin," my mom said to my stepdad, "I don't have anything to feed the kids tomorrow. What are we going to do?"

Even at nine years old, I knew times had been difficult. The year before, the family had moved three times, and there were job changes. I attended three different schools during third grade. Now, the family was back on the farm, but times were tough. The milk checks just weren't enough. Even at nine years old, I could tell that.

We had practically lived on cornmeal that winter. Cornmeal mush for breakfast. Cornmeal pancakes or Johnny Cake for supper.

The cornmeal pancakes showed up most often on the supper table. My mom was a wonderful and creative cook. She usually could put together a meal based on things most would question, and it would be good. But this winter was tough. There just wasn't anything to work with. Mom would get the can of dark syrup out of the cupboard and put it on the table. Using a table knife, she pried open the tin lid and put a tablespoon in the can. The spoon stood upright in the thick, cold syrup. The cupboards were mostly bare, but there was always dark syrup on hand. It was used in the baby's formula. The dark syrup wasn't one of my favorites. I much preferred the traditional thin and sweet pancake syrup, but that didn't fit in the family budget.

I was not a picky eater. I liked almost anything, but I had never cared much for cornmeal. By now, I was getting really tired of cornmeal. Cornmeal mush, cornmeal pancakes, and Johnny Cake, over and over. Often, we had cornmeal pancakes twice a day. We had it meal after meal, day after day that winter. At least it was something to eat, and it was filling. I don't remember any of us complaining. We just accepted it and ate it.

Our family had an elderly hired hand that winter. Ed was his name. He didn't require much. He worked for minimal wages and room and board. Ed wasn't a picky eater. He never complained either. If he had a thick slice of homemade bread dipped in bacon grease and drizzled with the dark syrup, he was happy. Ed ate plenty of cornmeal pancakes that winter, too.

Now it appeared even the cornmeal had run out. It's a scary thing for a young child to hear things like that and wonder where the next meal is coming from. For a child to hear their parents softly talking about their plan to be able to put food on the table is difficult.

As a child, I went to church and Sunday school. I knew of my Savior. I prayed daily. As I started to grow up too fast because of these challenges at home, I drew closer to God. Meanwhile, my mother and step-father went about their work the next day. I never told my parents that I overheard that conversation the night before. I went to school, came home, and food mysteriously appeared on the supper table. I didn't hear where the food came from, but I was grateful to have something to eat. It wasn't until much later that I learned where that food came from. During some of the worst of times, my parents would charge groceries by way of signing a note at the store or getting an advance on their milk check so they could buy groceries.

As a child, certain Bible stories stand out to you. God feeding the Israelites the daily manna as they wandered in the desert was a story that had made quite an impression on me. It became personal. I was in awe of how God provided food for the Israelites and what he provided them. As a little girl, I marveled at God's daily provisions of the manna every morning. I wondered about the taste of the manna. I had heard that it was sweet, and I liked that thought. The Bible says it tasted like something made with olive oil. "Surely, it tasted better than cornmeal pancakes and that awful dark syrup," I thought.

Now I look back to thoughts of the Israelites complaining that they didn't have enough to eat. Numbers 11 tells us they missed the variety of foods they had in Egypt. They missed having meat and fish and fresh produce. They whined and complained to Moses about the food situation. They started questioning why they had left Egypt to go to the Promised Land. God also provided quail for them, as well as the daily rations of manna six days of the week. I think about the Israelites wandering in the desert and eating the manna day after day. I think about the manna turning to maggots when they disobeyed the Lord and tried to keep extra when they weren't supposed to. Was God nudging them to trust that he would provide for them every day?

When I grew up and had a family of my own, I never forgot that humbling experience. I never forgot accidentally overhearing that my mom had nothing to feed the children the next day and no money with which to buy groceries. As we were raising our own little family, life would occasionally throw some challenges our way.

There were recessions and some long-term job layoffs. Money was sometimes tight, but we always got by. My heart wanted to worry, yet every time those challenges came along, I was comforted by God's provisions. Every time those challenges came along, God nudged me with memories of all the difficult times he had seen me through. He reminded me through his words, many sermons, and life events that he cares for his people. In doing so, he moved me to trust him to provide. He nudged me to let go of the worry, even though I wanted to cling to it.

Even all these decades later, I remember how hard it was eating those cornmeal pancakes meal after meal, day after day. But they filled me up. God's Word also filled me up. At a very young age, I learned how much God cares for us and will provide for us and protect us. When we are vulnerable, he is there. Always providing, always protecting, and ... yes, always filling us up!

* * *

... give me neither poverty nor riches,
but give me only my daily bread.
Otherwise, I may have too much
and disown you and say, 'Who is the Lord?'...

Proverbs 30:8,9 NIV

* * *

Pause to Ponder

Normally, young children would not be concerned about when and where their next meal is coming from. Not unless there is a problem or a lack of food. Then, it becomes a concern, perhaps even a worry. Even at a young age, God can show children how he takes care of us. He can show children that he sees the need and he provides. He may not always put a Rib-eye steak on the table or Apple Pie with ice cream, but he provides. As that child becomes an adult, that memory remains. It will always be there, wanting to manifest itself in worry during the next difficult times. But God remains also. He will always be there, nudging and reminding that adult of all the other times he met her needs. And when that worry wants to creep back in, he nudges her with a special and personal reminder. A reminder that he has never failed her.

Pause for Prayer

Dear Lord,

You have taught us so often that even when we have little, we are rich. We are rich in having a Savior who loves and cares for us. Help our hearts to focus on the heavenly riches you give to us, not the accumulation of earthly riches. You always give us just enough. We marvel at how you sometimes do these things in our lives. We know that you use these experiences to increase our faith. Thank you for seeing our needs and providing what we need when we need it. Help us to always remember that. Don't let us wander in our own desert complaining about what we don't have. Help us focus with thanksgiving on what we do have. Help us to keep our trust in you for what we need but don't have.

In Jesus's name.
Amen.

I am sure there must have been some instances in my adult life before this one. I was a young adult. I was a believer. I had faith, a fairly strong faith actually, but my faith was somewhat immature. I didn't always recognize God's hand in my life. I read the Bible. I had an active prayer life, but I needed to work on my relationship with God and letting him lead me in my life. The following story is what happened the first time I remember having a significant nudge as an adult.

CHAPTER 2

The Littlest Missionary

As a young married couple, we moved a lot. My husband, Jim, served in the Air Force. From 1970-1972, Jim was stationed in Okinawa, an island south of Japan in the East China Sea. Our first child, Lynn, was born there.

At the time we moved to Okinawa, the Vietnam War was in progress. Okinawa was still under American control and used American dollars. Prior to American control, a significant battle had been fought in Okinawa during WWll. The natives spoke Japanese. About six months after Lynn was born, the island reverted back to Japanese rule and returned to using Yen for currency. It is now considered to be part of Japan again.

At the time of Jim's tour, there was no internet available to the public. There was no YouTube. News wasn't as easily disseminated. It was screened, and some were censored. The Armed Forces TV network was six months behind in broadcasting American TV shows. It was only on for about six hours a day, and it repeated broadcasts. Sports lovers didn't get to see live games. There was no access to satellite TV. Mail was slow between the US and Okinawa. Having a phone installed in one's apartment was out of the price range of most of the young military families. Life felt somewhat isolated from the world.

Every day was an adventure. Living on an island and going to the beach year-round was such fun. My husband, being a young Airman First Class, didn't have enough rank to compete for base housing, so we lived on the local economy. Most of these people had so little. We lived in a modest new apartment building on top of a hill. I'm sure they considered us to be rich by their standards. The apartment was located off-base in what might have been considered a dividing point between the wealthy locals and the poor people. Looking out the balcony patio doors, we looked down on housing that was barely fit for livestock to live in. Small pieces of rusty tin roofs were pieced together to cover the botched together buildings. Looking out our front door, we saw people living in new apartment buildings and new single homes.

Many of the native people wore wide cone-shaped straw hats. For footwear, they mostly wore Geta (wooden sandals) or Zori tongs (straw sandals), which allowed them to slide across the road or floor instead of lifting their feet to take steps when they walked. The older women still wore kimonos. Some lived in thatch-roof homes. A few of the thatch-roof homes had TV antennas protruding from them, making for a strange landscape view among the rice and sugar cane fields.

Every day, I watched people pulling rickshaws in the streets below and people carrying heavy buckets on a pole over their shoulders. Occasionally there would be a couple of large pigs being herded down the road. Colorful backyard chickens were frequently seen picking seeds from the yard. Thriving green gardens appeared in any small patch of available land. Very small grocery stores dotted each neighborhood. They were attached to the owner's house. Women would often wrap their purchases in a large colorful cloth and carry them on their heads as they walked home.

We found it almost unbelievable, but in our apartment, our American style toilet had a diagram and instructions for use written in Japanese. Although we had indoor plumbing in our apartment, as we drove our car through the neighborhood, we kept it tight near the center of the road to avoid getting hung up in the sewage ditches that ran along each side of the road.

We immediately recognized what a blessing it was to come from a country that had so much in terms of modern conveniences, freedom, and safety.

We would sometimes go to the city of Koza or Naha to the open-air market. Memories of the sites and odors remain vivid to this day. Raw chickens were piled in huge aluminum dishpans in the hot sun, unrefrigerated, and uncovered. Odoriferous dried fish were stacked high on wooden shelves. Snack packs of dried seaweed stood where Americans would have displayed potato chips. High-pressure vendors were hoping to make a sale. On a good day, you might be able to bargain with them over the price of some children's clothing or some plastic wares.

Children were highly-esteemed in Okinawa. If you were in a store shopping, the sales ladies would ask to hold your child so you could look around and they could enjoy your little one.

One day, as we entered a gift shop, two sales clerks came running up to me with arms outstretched. They wanted to hold our daughter, Lynn. "Round eyes, blue eyes," they said as they giggled with glee. I felt a bit leery, but Jim kept an eye out while I shopped.

Everywhere we went, the Okinawans were drawn to our daughter. It was a society that loved children and respected and cared for the elderly. As I learned more about the culture, I was astounded to learn that only two percent of the natives were Christian at that time.

The native religion in Okinawa was a tribal religion that was animistic and shamanistic despite the fact that those beliefs varied. There was a great focus on assigning spirits to many things and worshipping those spirits. They believed that these spirits had an impact on their lives. Their religion stressed honoring the relationships between the dead and the living, including the gods and spirits in the natural world. Over time, their religion was believed to have been influenced by Shintoism, Buddhism, and Taoism. Those three religions came to Okinawa from contact with Japan and China. There was also a focus on ancestor worship. The result consisted of a mixture of religions and beliefs unique to the island.

A big three-day event, called the Obon Festival, was held every year in Okinawa. During Obon, a Buddhist celebration, they believed their ancestor spirits returned to the human world to visit their relatives.

There were Buddhist temples throughout the island. The more I learned about this, the more I felt a need to share the good news with some of these people. Had I just been nudged by God? There was a pull on my heart and conscience to do something, but what? I had no idea.

I taught Sunday school on base for the military children. Having come from an area of little diversity, I enjoyed the diversity of my class of fifth-graders. They did a class project to help people in other lands become independent enough to provide for their own day-to-day needs and earn a living. The children voted to raise money to buy chicks for the recipients to raise in another land. It was especially meaningful to the children, as they saw how poor many of the native Okinawans were.

Although I taught Sunday school to American children on base, I still thought about the 98% on the island who did not know Jesus. A familiar Bible verse went through my mind. "Go and make disciples of all nations…" But what could I do? Another nudge. When I read literature about the culture, I was reminded again about the 98%. Yes, nudged again!

Every time we took a drive, we would drive past one or more of the temples on the island. Each time I saw a temple, I was repeatedly reminded about the 98%. I ached for those people to know Jesus. Nudges, nudges, everywhere!

I didn't know how I could communicate the gospel with the locals. There was a language barrier. I didn't know how to speak Japanese. Oh sure, I could say some basic things to greet people and carry on sales transactions. It was difficult enough to communicate while paying rent and reporting problems with the apartment with the local landlords, who spoke no English. Having a six-month-old, I didn't have the time or access to take a course in Japanese. Still, it gnawed at my heart, knowing that these people were lacking in the good news of Jesus. With only three months left on the island, I was at a loss for how to respond to God's nudge.

One day as we explored the city, Jim went down an out-of-the-way side street. There wasn't much there and I wondered why we even bothered to go down that street. But suddenly, there it was—a small Lutheran book store. Nudged again! I had no idea there were any local resources available like this. We entered the shop and found tracts written in Japanese which shared the good news. Finally, I had my answer. I bought some tracts to take home.

The next challenge was how to distribute the tracts. By this time, we had moved to another area of the island. It was a nicer neighborhood with all newer homes. The neighbors here did not speak English either. One day, I decided it was time. God had placed me here on this island—this island with only two percent Christians. Over the years, I wondered how an average person could possibly help share the gospel around the world. Praying and giving to missionary work was about the only way most could help spread the Word at that time.

I had an opportunity before me. How could I approach this and be well-received long enough to give out the tracts? I thought about how I felt when people from other religions came to my house and wanted to change my beliefs. I worried I might not be welcomed by these strangers in a strange land. I prayed that God would allow this to happen.

I gathered up the tracts. I put my daughter in the stroller. I started walking down the street. Eventually, I stopped in front of a house. Picking up my daughter, I took a deep breath while walking up to the door of a stranger in this foreign land. And yet another Bible verse came to mind: "And surely I am with you always..." as I prayed "Thank you, Lord, I need you with me right now! I'm a little nervous."

Rap, rap, rap. I could hear the sound of the sliding wooden sandals heading towards the door. I took another deep breath. The door opened. The little Okinawan woman looked at the six-month-old "round-eyes, blue-eyes" and smiled. I smiled and said, "Konichiwa," which is Japanese for "Hello". The woman smiled back and reached out towards Lynn. She gently touched Lynn's chubby little fingers. I handed the little woman the tract bearing the precious cargo of the good news of Jesus Christ. The woman graciously accepted the tract. "Domo Arigato," she said, which means thank you very much in Japanese. "Douitashimashite," I replied, which means don't mention it, or you're welcome. I feebly attempted a couple more Japanese phrases, then smiled at the gentle little woman and said, "Sayonara."

Down the street we went, this nervous young American woman and her baby daughter. I smiled, greeted, and handed out tracts to passersby in between knocking on neighbor's doors until they were all gone.

Lynn and I went back to our apartment. Jim would soon be home from his shift as an air traffic controller at Kadena Air Base. I would tell him how our six-month-old daughter played her part as a missionary that day. For where language was a barrier, a cute little round-eyed, blue-eyed, blonde baby girl opened the door to communications and a sharing of the gospel. Years later, when my daughter was an adult, I told her about how she and I gave out the tracts that day. "You used me!" she said with a smile. I laughed. "Yes," I said. "I used you for the Lord."

❧

"Therefore go and make disciples of all nations, baptizing them in the name of the Father and of the Son and of the Holy Spirit, and teaching them to obey everything I have commanded you. And surely I am with you always, to the very end of the age."

Matthew 28:19-20 NIV

❧

Pause to Ponder

I will never know if those tracts yielded any fruit. I will never know if a seed was planted in any of the people we encountered or if they accepted Christ. But I do know that God called me to deliver those tracts that day. He repeatedly put it on my heart and nudged me to do so. I did not know how I would be able to have those encounters enabling that to happen. Somehow, I knew God would supply the way. I waited, knowing he would help me figure it out. And he did. He led me to the out-of-the-way Christian book shop. He showed me how the Okinawans loved little children, and I used that as the door opener. I prayed that those tracts would bring someone to Christ.

Pause for Prayer

Dear Heavenly Father,

Thank you for allowing us to live in a land with freedom of religion. Please guard that precious privilege. Thank you for allowing us to be exposed to your gospel in all of its truth. Let us never take that for granted. We pray that you would be with all the full-time missionaries as they go to lands near and far and bravely share your Word in sometimes hostile environments. Bless their efforts and keep them safe. Instill a burning desire in your new followers to learn more and stand strong in their faith. Give us the means to support those efforts, whether through our gifts, our prayers, or helping to spread your Word in our own humble way as missionaries where you have placed us. And as we do so, thank you, Lord, for being with us always.

In Jesus's name.
Amen.

CHAPTER 3

A Life-Changing Nudge

Retirement was getting closer. With that came a little apprehension. How was I going to adjust to retirement? I was a workaholic. I loved work. Fifteen years earlier, I had landed my dream job. I had a rewarding job teaching the soldiers and civilians of the Army Reserve. It took some time and experience for this older civilian woman to earn the respect of the younger students in the military and connect with them. I felt honored to be able to serve my country as a civilian, supporting our men and women in the military.

Gradually, over a period of time, work was getting difficult. I was exhausted all the time. Because of how I felt, the joy I previously felt while working was fading. My breathing was labored. I was diagnosed with allergy-induced asthma. I had trouble eating and trouble sleeping. I had pain in the joints and very itchy rashes. I also had Fibromyalgia and an enlarged liver. My husband and I were both having memory issues and problems concentrating. Our hearing was quickly declining. I was getting bad sinus infections. We both had eye irritation and blurred vision. We had trouble with headaches.

We weren't as sharp mentally as we used to be. My chest felt tight. It seemed as though I had to work harder to get a breath of air. I would hear my husband gasping for air at night. It was alarming. We were both exhausted all day long because we weren't sleeping well at night. Soon, we were to learn what all these symptoms meant.

Every year, when spring came and the tree buds started opening, I was in serious trouble. There would be a minimum of a two-week period where extreme fatigue caused me to sleep 14 hours a day. When I suffered from the worst of the breathing problems, nasal congestion, tight chest, and ear pain, I had to sit up in a recliner all night because of the coughing. This was followed by a sinus infection lasting two to three months. I would get very weak because I didn't have the strength to be up like usual. I had been sick for many years.

At work, most of our classes were taught at our state-of-the-art school located near my home. I also taught classes at various Army Reserve units throughout the lower 48 states, plus Alaska, Puerto Rico, Hawaii, Germany, and South Korea.

Although I loved instructing, it was a very draining job. Add to that the stress of travel and teaching at other sites added more challenges. Teaching a computer-based class using other people's equipment and networks increased the exhaustion factor. You planned and coordinated the best you could, but you never could be sure of what challenges you might encounter when dealing with other people's computer labs.

As the illness got worse, it became more and more difficult to keep my enthusiasm. I would be very nauseous in the morning. It's hard to project personality and add some humor to the class when you aren't feeling well. It's hard for co-workers to understand it, too. I didn't have the energy to deal with difficult personalities. I didn't have the energy to socialize or go out to lunch. I just wanted to do what I had to do at work, then go home and rest.

A couple of years before our school moved to another state, I was told that I had received the United States Army Reserve Civilian

Instructor of the Year Award. This was a nation-wide honor. I was told that my name and picture would be up on a LED display at the Headquarters of the organization giving the honor. They invited me to come to their Headquarters out east to receive the award at a big conference. It was truly a great honor, but my heart wasn't in it. I was feeling so sick. I just wasn't up for the trip. I had all I could do to make it to work every day. I didn't have the energy to do anything extra. I didn't know what to do. I didn't want to appear ungrateful. Finally, I decided that I just couldn't handle the trip. I had to decline. The award was presented to a representative of our organization. It was then brought home and presented to me locally. That was fine with me. Every aspect of my life was being impacted by this unending sickness.

I had been going to the doctor for several years for allergies. The tests revealed I was allergic to many foods, chemicals, environmental allergens, and many molds. Tests also revealed that I had candida. Candida is a strong overgrowth of yeast in your gut, caused by a fungus. It had a lot of nasty side effects.

The doctor explained that some people with allergies react immediately on exposure to their allergens, while other people are delayed reactors and may not notice symptoms until up to 24 or 48 hours after exposure. If I had allergies, that would make it challenging to figure it out on my own. The candida was one of my biggest problems. Treating it was going to cause me to feel worse temporarily. As the yeast died off, it released toxins, making people feel like they had the worst case of stomach flu ever. There would be chills, nausea, vomiting, body aches, bloating, gas, constipation, diarrhea, fatigue, dizziness, swollen glands, and muscle and joint pain. This would last two to four weeks. It could recur repeatedly as the candida symptoms came and went. The doctor also put me on an anti-fungal drug and a strict diet to try to help control the candida. The candida diet and the candida die-off made the first few weeks a challenge, as I felt worse than ever. I forced myself to go to work.

Candida overgrowth occurs when the immune system is weakened. The doctor recommended a good probiotic. He also recommended that I try to strengthen my weakened immune system. It is a delicate balance. The doctor told me that overuse of antibiotics was one of the culprits that brought on this condition. That also made sense, as I had been plagued with about three to four lengthy sinus infections per year. In other words, I was sick most of the year. Each sinus infection brought another prescription for antibiotics. Finally, I began to have some hope. Maybe I had found someone who could help.

The doctor prescribed sublingual antigen drops for part of my treatment. The effect was similar to getting allergy shots, only this could be done daily from home and would hopefully build up the resistance toward the allergens without having to go in for shots.

I was to avoid eating my allergic foods, especially when tree pollens and weed pollens were active. When the pollens were active the body's immune system went into overload and symptoms got worse than usual.

After about five years, the treatment was helping, but the allergies weren't yet under control. The asthma was not responding very well to treatment either. The breathing problems were gradually getting worse. My doctor felt fairly confident that when I retired, my allergy situation would improve. He felt the stress of working was the cause for the treatment taking so long to be fully effective. His insight made perfect sense to me. The thought of improved health made retirement sound even more appealing.

About one year before I retired, we started making preparations for retirement. We put an addition on our house. Our 840 square foot house was just too small when our son, daughter-in-law, and the grandchildren came home to visit. We added on a family room, a second bathroom, and an office. We also poured a patio slab and installed a new septic system. It was a major investment.

Finally, my retirement day arrived. I was hopeful we could resume a more normal social life after years of my husband working nights, weekends, and after his being on the road for a couple of years. We were looking forward to spending more time with our children and grandchildren. We were happy we would be entering retirement debt-free.

Unfortunately, we were too sick and too low on energy to socialize. We missed many social functions and felt like we were watching the world go by from our recliners. It became somewhat depressing. My allergy doctor thought I should be getting better after I retired, yet I seemed to be feeling worse.

I asked myself what was different. Why was I feeling worse? Suddenly, I realized it. I was home more! I had some concerns. I remembered that when I was still working, I often felt better when I would go away on work trips and be gone for one or two weeks. Why did I feel sicker when I spent more time at home? I had some concerns about mold. I started wondering again. We had already talked to two builders and two plumbers about this, and they all denied that we had mold. Oh sure, we had a few little spots on the paneling under the windows that had condensation during cold weather. We would clean that up and treat the wood, and that was the end of it until the next time. But deep in my heart, I knew that something just wasn't right, and I needed to get to the bottom of it. I still wondered about mold. My candida infection problem seemed to be getting worse, too. I learned that in people with weakened immune systems, candidiasis can be life-threatening. This can happen if it passes into the bloodstream and spreads to important organs.

As we go through life's challenges, we often try to fix things ourselves. We don't always turn to God first for help. And then God nudged me. I realized it was long past time for me to turn this all over to the Lord. As I was feeling sicker and sicker, I prayed that God would enlighten me. This was more than I was prepared to deal with by myself. I prayed that he would help me to find out what was wrong and show me what to do.

I started doing research online. I made phone calls. After doing the allergy testing, I knew that I was highly allergic to several kinds of mold. It seemed to make sense to follow up on this. We hired an environmental hygienist to do mold testing and a property and building analysis to identify any other issues that might relate to mold and water damage. They tested the air outside the house, inside the house on the main floor, and in the basement. They did analysis and comparisons of the readings. The test results were very revealing.

Our home testing disclosed high numbers of several kinds of mold contamination both on the main floor and in the basement. Although we were most concerned about the black mold, the biggest concern of the environmental hygienist was our aspergillus mold levels. An aspergillus test of 36,000 indicates mold contamination in homes. The count in our home was over 100,000. Aspergillus produces aflatoxin, which is one of the most potent naturally occurring carcinogens. This would be a serious health risk.

The environmental hygienist told us it was not safe to continue living in our house. We had to either demolish and rebuild the old house or leave the house forever. Clearly, we had some big decisions to make. We were devastated.

We thought about our recent substantial investments in our place. We had already paid for it all out of our retirement savings.

On inspection, the environmental hygienist told us our one and one-half year old addition was not infected with mold. It would be able to be salvaged, if we decided to rebuild our house. Thank you, Lord, for that!

I found a few books about mold and illnesses caused by mold. One was written by a couple who had survived Hurricane Katrina. It was very helpful. I knew we were facing something very serious, and that we had to do something. All my research was confirming that.

Much to my surprise, I found that even the Bible had some things to say about mold. In Leviticus 14:33-46, we find detailed instructions on how to deal with mold in a home. One of the books I read about mold and mold illness mentioned some of these Bible verses. It was encouraging to find these Bible verses in a secular book. How amazing to know that God cares so much about us that he gives us all this information within the Bible. He even shares things to help us with our health and everyday living. Reading this in the Bible really spoke to me about our situation and what we needed to do.

As I read the Bible verses mentioned in the book, it also brought to mind another biblical concept: Matthew 6:19. "Do not store up for yourselves treasures on earth, where moths and vermin destroy and where thieves break in and steal."

If we decided to build, the new house did not have to be fancy. It did not have to be nicer than the neighbor's. It did not have to be a mansion to impress, filled with all the finest furnishings. It just had to be functional, healthy, and comfortable. After all, this home was only going to be temporary. Our forever home was what mattered most. That heavenly home we all longed for was still to be our focus.

One of the things these books about mold impressed me with was that mold doesn't have to be visible to be present. And that was our situation. Our home inspection and analysis revealed that. Most of our mold was hidden, out of sight, buried behind walls, under windows, under a past leaky roof prior to our occupancy, in between our paneling and the exterior siding, and in the basement. We saw very little mold.

There are several ways molds can impact our health. When you inhale, touch, or ingest any of these mold spores, you can expose and affect many different systems and organs within your body. Exposure to these molds can cause infections. They weaken people's immune systems so they can't fight off other illnesses they are exposed to. This also made sense in our situation. We were constantly sick. We would just get rid of a cold, sinus infection, or flu, and we would catch something else.

With compromised immune systems, we had to be very careful. We would catch common colds and viruses easily and be very sick for a long time. We curtailed being out in public during cold and flu outbreaks. We missed a lot of church in the winter. When possible, we tried to avoid so many people. We tried to avoid shaking hands. We tried to go to the store in the very early morning hours to avoid being around a lot of people. I had to use double-strength Netti Pots twice a day to help with the sinus congestion and pain.

In the midst of all this, my husband had his annual physical. Sadly, some test results revealed some areas of concern. "You're going to need a biopsy," they told him. The biopsy confirmed that he had cancer. How could this be happening? "How much more?" I thought. "How are we going to do all this?" I had to wonder, was my husband's cancer caused by the mold?

These molds produce fungal spores. The way my allergy doctor explained it, these tiny invisible spores have the equivalent of suction cups on them and can stick to things quite easily. Certain molds can have a second impact on humans. For example, aspergillus, which was our highest mold count, produces a mycotoxin. A mycotoxin is just as it sounds. It is a toxin. But this toxin is one produced by a fungus. Mold is a fungus.

The toxin that aspergillus produces is an aflatoxin. This known carcinogen can cause liver disease and cancer. Aflatoxin is so dangerous that it has even been weaponized for use in war.

Studies revealed alarming statistics. People who were ill from toxic exposure to aspergillus were said to have aspergillosis. Studies showed that even though patients with invasive aspergillosis took strong antifungal drugs and had hospital treatment, 50% to 99% of patients with a compromised immune system died. Cancer, which my husband had, can weaken the immune system. Candidiasis, which I had, can also affect your immune system. Candidiasis is a fungal infection caused by a yeast (a type of fungus) called candida. It can cause severe problems in the intestinal tract. I had been taking an anti-fungal medication for several years for intestinal candidiasis, and I was getting sicker. Clearly, our health was on the line.

Mycotoxins can produce disease. They can cause heart problems and sinus problems. I had a long history of sinus infections. They suppress people's immune systems, making them more susceptible to getting contagious illnesses easily and having difficulty in fighting illness off. It can mimic pneumonia. It can damage the liver. I had infectious hepatitis when I was six years old, which impacts the liver. I turned yellow. I missed about one month of school. As an adult, I was diagnosed with an enlarged liver, so I used caution about what I consumed in order to protect my liver. I started noticing that even after an occasional half glass of wine on a special occasion, I would vomit. Eventually, I learned that the overgrowth of yeast goes crazy when any kind of alcohol is consumed. It was not worth getting sick over it. I decided I should not have any kind of alcoholic beverages.

Exposure to the mold mycotoxins can cause vision problems, hearing problems, memory loss, and depression. Chronic fatigue and anxiety can also come as a result of exposure to the mycotoxins produced by the mold. We were both very fatigued all of the time.

For the past seven years I had been experiencing swollen glands in my neck...all the time. This, also, struck me as rather strange. Clearly, my body was constantly fighting something.

Asthma is often a result of this exposure also. I had Asthma. Although I had an inhaler, it didn't seem to do much to help with my breathing. I was noticing more and more shortness of breath. Going up and down stairs was becoming a real problem.

Eventually, more testing using an ultra-sound revealed an additional diagnosis of pulmonary hypertension. It affects both the lungs and the heart. I was having dizziness and heart palpitations.

This affects the arteries in people's lungs. It also affects part of the heart because it has to work harder due to constricted or damaged blood vessels in the lungs. This, in turn, weakens the heart muscle. There are several kinds of pulmonary hypertension, and it has no cure. That explained why walking fast in the airport to catch a plane made me feel like my lungs were about to burst. That also explained why I often couldn't get enough air to sing hymns in church.

Another alarming revelation was that mold can also impact your ability to reason and think clearly. How could we make a decision about what to do when we couldn't even think clearly?

It seemed before we made any major decisions, we needed to find out how much the insurance would cover. We filed an insurance claim. It was denied. A couple of years prior, Hurricane Katrina had occurred. They told us that following Hurricane Katrina, the insurance companies quit paying for mold claims for homes. How could this be? Were we not going to be compensated a thing for the loss of our house and much of its contents? We were just expected to take this loss with no reimbursement. Wasn't this why we paid for homeowner's insurance? Most of what we owned was about to be going in a dumpster with no reimbursement.

We were sick, aging, and losing most of what we owned. I was already retired and too sick to go get another job. Jim was still working, but I could see he was struggling. He needed to retire, but he felt he needed to keep working because of the situation at hand. It felt similar to when we got married, and we were starting out with nothing; only then were we young and had our health and earning potential ahead of us. By now, we were 64 and 65. Our earning potential and our health were going. We felt like we had lost everything…well, almost. We still had God. We still had our faith. We still had our loved ones.

We were devastated. I cried. Together, we prayed like never before. We didn't know what to do. It seemed there were no good options.

Now I don't know of too many women who wouldn't be excited at the possibility of getting a new house and new furniture. Normally, that is an exciting time. Normally. I was having trouble getting excited about getting this new house because of being sick, all the work that lie ahead, and the heavy financial burden this was going to be.

As we thought about this, we were emotionally drained. Most people our age had their homes paid for as they entered retirement. Most people our age who bought or built a new house had a house to sell, which they could use for a big down payment. If someone's home was destroyed by a tornado, they generally had an insurance claim with reimbursement for their home. Not so for us. It was all a total loss for us. Most people our age had already bought and paid for their furniture, clothes, and bedding before they retired. Not so for us.

After all this research, it was getting close to the holidays. We weren't going to be able to move out until spring. Regardless of our decision, we had to move out. Even if we decided to rebuild, we could not stay in the saved portion of the house when construction was going on. When the warm weather came, the mold would be more active in the old portion of the house, so we had to be out of the house by then.

We realized this was a lot to process and a major decision. We felt completely overwhelmed. We were trying to figure this out on our own. And then God nudged us. He used sermons, and he used Bible verses. His timing is always amazing. He reminded us to turn to him during these times of crisis in our lives. And the prayers kept coming.

Dear Lord, We ask for your help as we face these difficult decisions. Please lead us in the way we should go. We have so many things to consider. We feel so over-whelmed. Please make it obvious what we should do in order to protect our health. Please give us the strength to do what we must do. We ask these things in Jesus's name. Amen.

We went on a fact-finding mission. We were so devastated we couldn't even bring ourselves to talk to very many people about all this to seek advice. We prayed, asking God to provide us the information we needed to help us make an informed decision.

There was much to consider as we made our decision. We had to look at our budget. We were still adjusting to my retirement annuity. We had just spent a large chunk of our retirement savings on our addition. We had already considered our health and knew that doing nothing was not an acceptable option.

We looked into listing our old home to sell it. The realtor said they no longer listed modular homes. We thought of selling it on our own. We wondered, "Who would want to buy 1/3 of a house? A house that didn't even have a kitchen or a bedroom?" We also thought about how few people would be willing to take a chance on our new addition. Would they be worried that it would also have issues? Would they believe us that the inspector said the addition was mold-free? How would we ever recoup our recent investment in our property? Would buyers expect us to practically give it away because of the circumstances? At least if we rebuilt our old house, we would be keeping our investment in the new addition.

I started looking for an apartment or house to rent in the spring. Almost all of them required renters to sign a one-year lease. We surely hoped we would not need a rental property for that long. Finally, I found an apartment and a landlord who was willing to work with us on the lease. It was close to our building site. Unfortunately, I found some mold in the apartment, too. Surely, it had to have less mold than in our home. With nothing else available, we signed a six-month lease and trusted God to take care of us in the apartment.

There were so many decisions to make. Should we sell? Walk away? Rebuild the main part of the house? Jim said he was not ready to live in an apartment yet on a permanent basis. He also didn't want to walk away from the big investment we had just made in our property.

I didn't know how we would deal with the physical aspects of rebuilding. We were both very sick. We had no energy. We were exhausted all the time. Physically, could we handle this between being sick and our advancing age?

With the house ordeal, we incurred additional expenses. At the recommendation of the environmental hygienist, we hired a mold remediation service to clean the basement and ductwork. We had to replace linens, towels, sheets, pillows, and any infrequently worn clothes that might be contaminated. All the upholstered furniture had to go according to my allergy doctor. The bedroom set had black mold on the back of the headboard and the back of the chest and dresser, so it also had to go. No wonder we couldn't breathe at night! The coffee and end tables were too big for our future smaller living room. Most of the furniture had to go, and of course, now there would be payments for the new house. I worried about it.

All this while, God was nudging me. As I read my devotions, he reminded me through numerous Bible verses that I needed to trust in him. After my initial shock wore off, I tried to put more and more faith in his promised provisions. Surely, our God is a good God. Surely, he is going to take care of us through this.

As the gravity of the financial impact on us was revealed, our hearts sank. I felt I should go back to work, but I was too sick to do so. Besides, someone had to be available to coordinate all this house stuff.

As construction began, we would be paying apartment rent and payments on the construction loan at the same time. Our grocery bill soared as we had to buy as much organic food as we could afford to so that we could attempt to relieve some of the toxic burden on our overloaded immune systems.

While we were dealing with all this, there was another concern at the back of my mind. We didn't even own a decent vehicle. Our truck and car were both old and questionable. They both needed replacing. I was driving a 16-year-old car. My husband had wanted to get me a newer car several times over the past few years. I had declined a replacement car several times, telling him I'd rather wait until retirement so that we would enter retirement with a good, newer vehicle. Jim was driving a 13-year-old high-mileage truck, which he had used for a business a few years earlier. We had talked of getting different vehicles right after I retired. With all the sickness, mold testing, and follow-up, we just hadn't gotten it taken care of yet. Now winter was approaching. I thought about Jim's cancer. What if we have to travel out of town for him to get treatments this winter? We would need a dependable vehicle for that. Somehow, with all we have going on, we need to go vehicle shopping and get a good car.

Jim looked off and on for the next four months and eventually found a good car for a reasonable price. I continued to drive the old car just for local errands. A few months later, our old car broke down. It was beyond the point of repair. We donated it to a charity. As we watched the charity pick-up trailer haul it away, we marveled at God's timing.

We needed estimates for the bank, which meant we needed to find a builder to give us those estimates. I prayed for God to guide us to the right builder. After all, we had already been told by two plumbers and two carpenters that we didn't have mold. We needed to have someone we knew, someone we could trust, and someone who would acknowledge mold and work towards our having a safe new home.

This was not going to be easy. The housing industry had been having a slow-down. We knew many builders. We didn't want to slight anyone. There weren't a lot of building jobs at this time. But we needed to ensure we had the right person for our situation. I knew builders from work. We had builders in our congregation at church. We had builders in the family. We knew they all were good. Once again, we looked to prayer.

Please God, guide us in choosing the right builder. We know many good builders, but please send us the right builder for our job. Please send us someone who will respect and recognize the significance of dealing with mold and mold prevention. This is a one-shot deal, Lord. We can't afford any mistakes. We can't afford a re-do if it goes wrong. We are on a fixed income. We need to do this correctly. We need someone we can trust.

Jim's cousin was a builder. He had been doing this for many years. We were confident he and several others we knew were fully capable of doing the job. It seemed his cousin would be a logical choice. Before we asked him about the job, we were told (incorrectly, we later learned) that his cousin was no longer building houses. We knew that he had fallen off a roof and was badly injured. He was in a lot of pain. We wondered now what to do. We didn't want him to feel as though he needed to take the job just to help us out if he really wasn't feeling up to it. We were concerned it would be too much for him. We also didn't want to slight anyone we knew. In reality, we had one job. We could only choose one builder. We continued to pray about it and trusted God to lead us to the answer.

Over the next few weeks, one name came up repeatedly. He was married to a relative. I knew his wife had mold allergies and had experienced bad reactions to mold. They knew and understood, to a degree, what we were dealing with.

Scott was a builder. He was not an expert in mold, nor did we expect him to be. We had already talked to the mold experts. We knew that Scott understood the impact of mold because of what his wife had experienced. Our ongoing concern was always playing through our minds after having those two plumbers and two carpenters do work in our home, and all denied that we had mold in our home. It was important to us to have a builder that we knew understood the impact of mold and the significance of building to avoid future mold in every way possible. Was he to be our builder? We prayed more about it and felt God leading us to ask Scott to do the job.

We got a bid from Scott for rebuilding and talked to the bank about loans. We knew our budget would get even tighter once Jim retired, so we went with the figures for the 30-year loan. That was when the reality hit from the impact of our circumstances. If we lived that long, we would be 94 and 95 when we paid off the new house!

We hired Scott to build the house. Scott did a lot of research. He came to zoning committee meetings with us. He talked to contractors to help us do things in the new house that would alleviate problems we had encountered in the past. He talked to contractors about getting us a quality air system. He researched and consulted with others about many issues on the exterior that could be addressed as well. What a blessing to have someone willing to put in so much extra effort for our situation. We were so thankful.

As we went through this process, we had to acknowledge that God is good. He strengthened our faith. He helped us see what is really important in life. What we were losing were all just things. Our faith, our health, our relationships…those were the important things. Although our health was in question at this point, our relationships were strong, and our faith was strong. God was providing guidance and his comfort every step of the way. We didn't know how this would turn out, but we knew with confidence that God would get us through this. His Word assured us of that.

Time passed, and on two occasions over the next few months, I saw a car sitting on the edge of the road, taking pictures of our house. I was a bit concerned and told my husband about it. A month or so after the second instance, we got a letter from our insurance company saying they were dropping our homeowners insurance. What? How could that be? We were going to rebuild. We had told them that previously. We were still paying our premiums. They never called us to discuss this or ask questions. They just were going to drop our coverage with no prior communication.

We had to have a meeting and explain once again that we were looking into rebuilding, but it takes time to research, plan, hire a contractor, and get on their schedule. We had the mold evaluation done in August. It was October by the time we got the full written analysis back. It was too late then to get on a contractor's schedule for that fall. Even though we had told them we were going to rebuild, the insurance company assumed that because nothing visible was happening outside, we weren't going to do anything. We contacted the insurance agent. The company kept us on.

While doing all the research, coordination, and decision-making, I also tried to mentally prepare myself for the changes to come. There would be lifestyle adjustments and more to prepare for. God was nudging me to examine my heart. I needed to get past the anger and disappointment about a lack of reimbursement from our insurance. I needed to get past the questions about why this happened. I needed to continue to thank God for providing answers to our health dilemma and giving us a chance to do something about it.

I needed reminders that God was there with us. He was going to see us through this. He was going to provide. He was going to give us strength. He did still love us. He did not have plans to harm us. That's why he led us to solve the puzzle on why we were so sick.

I had a stack of devotion books that I used for my early morning readings. I had some home decor with Bible verses on them. I put them out where I could see them often. I was still stressing over the financial aspects of all this. Lifestyle adjustments weren't very appealing. Neither was taking on a big loan at this point in life. My husband always wanted to pay cash for everything in the past. This was not an option now. Within six months, we were about to build a new house, buy two newer vehicles, and replace our furniture, our bedding, most of our clothing and linens, and much of the contents of our old house. Yes, we were now going to be in debt as we entered retirement. This was something we had worked to avoid. I knew I had to get in a better frame of mind concerning that. It was dragging me down.

Things had been so busy as we researched everything. We were so exhausted. It was hard to keep up with normal day-to-day living, along with all the extra work we had to do right now. I knew we needed to be in the Bible right now and praying. Yet, we were so exhausted; it was easy to say, "We'll do our devotions later when the work is done." Then, when the work was done, we were so tired all we wanted to do was grab a bite to eat and go to bed. I knew we had to do better. How could we expect God to do his best for us when we weren't doing our best for him? We had to prioritize our time with the Lord. Despite the exhaustion. Despite the stress. Despite the sickness. I looked to God's word, and I prayed. One of the things I prayed about was how we were going to pay for this new house and everything else we needed to replace.

The Lord led me to James 4:2 NIV. *"You desire but do not have, so you kill. You covet but you cannot get what you want, so you quarrel and fight. You do not have because you do not ask God."* The beginning of this verse did not seem to apply, but the last line struck me. "… *You do not have because you do not ask God."* I felt rather foolish. We had been so focused on all the obstacles, all the challenges, all the expenses, and the feelings of this just not being attainable. I looked back. We were praying, but what were our words? Had we even asked God to give us a new house? Were we showing God that we had faith that he would do this for us?

Then I pondered. I tried to look at our situation objectively. Was God trying to punish us? I didn't believe so. What was the Lord's purpose in all this? I knew in my heart that he wanted nothing but good for us.

❧

"For I know the plans I have for you," declares the Lord,
"plans to prosper you and not to harm you,
plans to give you hope and a future."

Jeremiah 29:11 NIV

❧

Did I believe that God could make this happen for us? Yes, I did.

❧

Jesus looked at them and said,
"With man this is impossible, but not with God;
all things are possible with God."

Mark 10:27 NIV

❧

That led me to examine my heart. Do I believe that God will make this happen for us?

❧

"Therefore I tell you,
whatever you ask for in prayer,

believe that you have received it, and it will be yours."

Mark 11:24 NIV

I knew that I had to think in different terms. This IS happening. God IS taking care of us. He IS providing the way. He IS clearing out the obstacles. The question was, could we hold up to all this with our failing health? And then, just like always, he provided the reminder I was seeking.

I can do all this through him who gives me strength.

Philippians 4:13NIV

So often, the answers are in the Bible—our manual for life. Do we look there for the answers when we are going through our most challenging times?

I needed to draw on God's strength. He would see us through this. God had nudged me with his Word. I had just been reminded of how God's Word refreshes us. It adjusts our mindset.

I wanted to keep some reminders in front of me for the challenging days ahead. I made a sign on my computer. I put "Dare to Ask" at the top of a page and inserted a picture of a modest ranch-style house similar to what we were going to build. Below it I put an excerpt of James 4:2 NIV, "…You do not have, because you do not ask God." It was a reminder to keep praying and asking God. I printed it, framed it, and put it where we would see it every day. It was to be a reminder to ask God for what we needed and to have faith that he would give us what we needed. I still have that printout.

We needed to submit ourselves to God and trust. I knew we shouldn't be asking for things just because we wanted them according to this Bible verse, but I understood that it was permissible to ask for what we needed. Instead of worrying and stressing about it, why weren't we taking the next step and asking God to give us what we needed? At first, it felt uncomfortable asking God for a new house. It seemed a bit extreme…a bit extravagant.

God has his ways of confirming things for us and this was no exception. I later read more reassuring words. The more I read the Bible, the more that he revealed to me. There were so many nuggets of gold buried within these pages, waiting to be discovered, or perhaps rediscovered.

✧

"Until now you have not asked for anything in my name.
Ask and you will receive, and your joy will be complete."

John 16:24 NIV

✧

He who did not spare his own Son,
but gave him up for us all—

how will he not also, along with him,
graciously give us all things?

Romans 8:32 NIV

⁓

It was going to be alright. God was going to help us get the house
that we needed. All we had to do was ask. Ask in Jesus's name, and
we will receive. Not only would we receive, but we would have joy.
That sounded like something to look forward to. There hadn't been
much joy lately. Thank you, Lord, for that. It was not too much to
ask of God. After all, he had already sacrificed his Son for us. How
could a new house compare with that?

We had been so busy, so upset, so overwhelmed, so exhausted, so
sick, and so down that we had neglected to turn to God first. When
we needed him most, we looked everyplace except where we should
have looked. Please forgive us, Heavenly Father.

As winter set in, we worked on all the behind-the-scenes things
required. We submitted our request for variance zoning packets to
the township and the city Extra Territorial Zoning Committee. We
looked into the building permits. We prepared to move out of the
house and into the apartment. We looked into moving companies and
storage units. We gathered up containers for packing and moving.
Cleaning out the house and basement were projects we needed to
get started on.

By spring, things were getting busy. We moved into the apartment
in June and continued working on emptying the house out. In July,
we had record-breaking heat. Almost every day that month exceeded
ninety degrees. While Jim was at work, I was spending most of my
time in the basement. I had to go through totes and decide what we
would keep versus what we'd get rid of. The heat and humidity were

making the mold out of control. To protect from mold exposure, we were supposed to wear goggles and gloves in the basement as we did this, but the heat was causing our glasses to fog up and condensation to drip down the lenses. It was miserable, and it was to the point of being dangerous. We were not able to see properly. Finally, we had to stop wearing the goggles. After the sorting, we hauled dumpster items outside. We threw away two large dumpsters full of our belongings. Some items we washed and disinfected to keep, and some we put in the storage units for cleaning later. The more exposure to the mold, the sicker we got.

We got the building permit before Labor Day and shifted our focus to construction. On demolition day, our old house was in dumpsters by 11:30 AM. I prayed the construction crew would remain safe and not get exposed to any bad stuff from the demolition. The days soon became filled with trips to the construction site, consults with the builder, and trips to the building supply stores to pick out all the things associated with building a house.

Although my days were full, my nights were full too. I was writing a book…two, actually. Several years prior, I had applied for a trademark name for a series of books. Not knowing what was to come in the future, I had a time frame in which to get these two books published so I could secure and finalize my trademark. With all the sickness and dealing with all the house business, I was nearing the deadline. If I didn't get my two books published by a specific date in October, I would lose my trademark. I looked at the calendar and hung my head. With just three weeks to finish two books, I felt like giving up.

How could I possibly finish one book and write another in that amount of time while keeping everything moving on the new house? I was still sick and exhausted. I was ready to give up on the book and the trademark. It had all just become too much. I felt depleted, like I had nothing left to give. Nothing left to draw on.

One morning, the phone rang. It was the company that was filing my trademark paperwork for me. They encouraged me to go through with the books. They said, "You have such a good trademark name. It would be a shame to give it up." How likely is it that a company that files trademarks would call a customer to encourage them to pursue this? Was this another nudge? I still felt very defeated and hopeless about accomplishing the goal. But…I looked at the status of the partially done book. The other book was going to be easier, and I had done some piecemeal work on some of it. I tried for a week to get something done on it. But by this point, there was so much going on with the house that I was facing frequent interruptions and frequent trips to the building site. I talked to our builder. I asked him if he could give me two weeks with no calls or interruptions to make decisions or come to the building site so I could focus 100% on writing. He said yes, and I finished the books!

I sent the books off for a priority job on the formatting. They were formatted and ready for me to publish just a couple of hours before the deadline for my losing my trademark! I still do not know how I accomplished that. Truly, God was looking out for me as I typed until the early morning hours and stayed up all night the night before I published it. Then, when I should have been so happy and relieved, for some reason, I felt no joy when I clicked the last button on the screen that said: "PUBLISH." What was wrong? Why was I feeling kind of down and as if something just wasn't right, when I should have been ecstatic that I had met my deadline?

The next day, after I published the book, we decided to take a drive to a favorite restaurant about an hour away. It was time to celebrate the completion of the books by the deadline. On the way home, my cell phone started ringing like crazy. I had numerous messages. I didn't know what to think. One by one, I went through the messages. Each one revealed a little information, but I still didn't know the entire story. And then I heard the most shocking message of all, "We are planning on going to the funeral." I still didn't know for sure whose funeral it was. Eventually, I found out that, unknown to me, one of my brothers, living on the other side of the country, had been killed in a horrific head-on cycle accident. It happened just two hours after I published the books. Could this have been why I didn't feel any joy when I pushed the publish button?

My brother was riding with one of his cycle riding groups when a reckless driver hit several cyclists in his group. "How much more?" I thought. "How much more can we deal with all at once?"

I flew to the coast for my brother's celebration of life. There were about 400 people there. He was loved by many. With a hole in my heart, I returned home and continued to work on all the decisions that go into building a house.

All this while, we were working through the house ordeal we had other things going on in our lives. It seemed there was so much to deal with all at once.

My mother-in-law had experienced a major stroke. She and her bachelor brother, who lived with her, ended up going into a nursing home. With her stroke came depression. She cried a lot. They tried so many different anti-depressants. Nothing seemed to help. Her brother, my husband's uncle, was also lonely and wanted visitors and help with things. I tried to help as much as I could with them, as Jim was still working full time and then coming home and helping with the house preparation work. We were physically and mentally exhausted. It was too much. Once again, God, in his wisdom and care, saw that we needed a break. He provided some relief. He sent us a volunteer. A retired hospice nurse went to visit Jim's mother once a week to give us a break from having to go quite so often until we were done with the house. We hadn't been looking for someone to do this. The nursing home staff just told us about it one day. The volunteer drove over a half hour each way when she came to visit her. We were so thankful.

Even so, the challenges continued. Nurses would call when Jim would be at work. A concerned voice on the other end of the phone said, "Your mother-in-law is crying. She is lonely. Even though she has been getting company, she thinks no one has been here to see her for a long time. Can you come to see her now?" This would be when I was struggling to get done what I had to do while not feeling well. So, I would stop what I was doing and go to visit her. She had suffered a stroke, had severe depression, and had dementia, along with a host of health problems. Some days, I got things done for the house. Some days I didn't.

As I continued selecting things for the house, I started looking at materials for a kitchen backsplash. Looking at the sample boards, I noticed a beautiful accent tile. I liked the design; the colors were perfect, and something seemed familiar about it. I soon realized it looked just like the ichthus—the Christian fish symbol, or as some call it, the Jesus fish. I didn't know if the designer intentionally made them appear to be the Christian fish symbol or if it was just by coincidence that it looked like it. I learned that this was a secret symbol used by early Christians to identify themselves as followers of Jesus.

I found some reasonably priced tiles to use as my backsplash that would complement the fish tiles nicely. I was excited to think that I would have a beautiful reminder in my kitchen--the room I spent so much time in--of the one who got us through the entire house ordeal. It seemed so perfect!

When I decided to order the fish tiles, I was met with disappointment. "Sorry, that style has been discontinued," the sales associate said. I couldn't believe it. Every store I went to said it was no longer being made or offered. I started thinking about the sample boards still having the fish tiles on display. I went to various stores and asked if they would sell me their sample fish tiles. I really wanted these accent tiles! Some sold them to me. Others gave them to me. I went back to my original store to ask the same. The sales associate was so nice, she gave it to me. Over a period of a few weeks, she kept locating a few tiles here and there. Finally, she called. There would be enough accent tiles that I could use the fish tile accent!

I thought they were beautiful and it would be a wonderful reminder of God's active hand in our move to a healthy house. It was amazing how I got those tiles…piece by piece! It was so touching that this sales associate spent so much time and effort searching for these tiles so I would have enough. It meant a lot to me to have that reminder in my kitchen.

Things started falling into place. Our builder gave up some of his much-cherished deer-hunting to help meet the goal. The house was finished a few days before Christmas in 2013. Our daughter and son-in-law helped move some things. The moving truck pulled up to our apartment. They loaded up our belongings and brought them home. Home to the same address, but a different house. Home to a new and healthy house.

We had no Christmas tree and no decorations. They had all gone in the dumpster. The next day, I bought a new artificial Christmas tree and ninety-nine-cent packages of red and gold Christmas balls. I stopped at a craft store and purchased a few Christmas centerpieces at 75% off to add a splash of color to our otherwise barren house. A couple of days later, our son, daughter-in-law, and two grandchildren arrived on the 23rd of December. My daughter-in-law washed dishes and put them away. Our son helped with various odd jobs. Furniture was sparse and would be for a few months, but that was okay, as we were all together with them and our daughter and son-in-law.

Two days later, we celebrated Christmas in our new healthy house. I cooked my first holiday meal in our new kitchen. As I did so, I looked at the fish tiles in complete amazement at what God had just gotten us through.

Now that we had moved into our new house, we were able to start to have a little social life once again. "Well, it's over now. You're out of the moldy house and in your new house," people would say. But… they didn't understand. Yes, the work was done. Yes, we were living in the new house, but we were doing so still in our old, sick bodies. It was exhausting trying to explain it to people. It was complicated. It was more information than most people wanted to hear. Because it was complicated, it was difficult for them to process.

We wanted them to know the truth, yet we didn't want to come across as complainers. God hates complaining. Often, the easiest way to handle it was to just ignore it and go along with their assumptions that we were okay. Don't get me wrong. Thankfully, we had experienced some improvements, but we were not "okay." I still had lots of breathing issues, including asthma. We both had very weak immune systems. We caught colds and flu easily. I still had ongoing and long-lasting sinus infections. When either of us did get sick, it usually hung on for weeks, often months. Everything was playing off of each other. The fungal overgrowth was feeding the mold sickness. They were both feeding the sinus infections. The sinus infections required antibiotics. The antibiotics kept the endless cycle going. The seasonal allergies would multiply the impact of fungal overgrowth and mold sickness. It was a never-ending cycle because of our weakened immune systems.

Before moving back home, I had found some nice used furniture replacements. I now started looking for more quality used furniture. They were few and far between. Most were a distance away. Slowly, we found more. We waited for our local furniture store's semi-annual upholstered furniture sale and ordered a new sofa, recliners, and side chairs. Several months after we moved into the house, we finally had all of our furnishings.

We were now in a situation where we could actually invite company.

Now, some might wonder if I am bitter about what has happened. Do I wonder why this happened? Do I feel God was punishing us? No, no, and no. This is life. God always has a plan. Sometimes, we may be able to understand what it was all about, and other times, we may not. I am thankful we are finally living in a healthy house. I am thankful there is no more mold. I am thankful God supplied what we needed when we needed it. I am thankful God used this experience to draw us closer to him. To help us learn to trust in him.

Although we still have health issues related to mold, we are thankful for the progress we have made. We still have weakened immune systems. We still have to be very careful about being exposed to illness and mold. We still get sick and take weeks or months to recover from infections. Our immune systems still can't fight off illness. We pray that God will improve our health more. In order to avoid contagious germs, we still hesitate to shake hands during the flu and cold season.

I look back on the entire sequence of events and am truly amazed at how God got us through all that. There were so many difficult things to deal with all at once in our life. There were so many challenges, obstacles, and hurdles. It was such a puzzle to figure out the entire mold and health problem situation. The fact that mold impacts people's memory and their ability to think clearly and reason made this very challenging. It is amazing that we were able to figure it all out. There were so many steps to getting out of the old house, rebuilding, and back into the new house. Even after ten years, there continues to be an ongoing process in the detox journey to heal our bodies, minds, and health.

We never could have figured it all out on our own. Yet God was there for us, helping us find our way through this maze of challenges. He provided a wealth of information, and we saw his hand at work throughout the process: The clues about our illness helped us learn what was going on. Finding some very nice used furniture to save us a little money. The phone call from the Trademark Company to encourage me not to give up on my books. The timing of my notification of my brother's death—after I clicked the publish button. Had it been earlier, I likely wouldn't have been able to focus enough to finish the book by the deadline. God nudged us every step of the way. How blessed we are!

Yes, I have lived a blessed life. God's been good to me. He's given me everything I need. And I have come to realize that I do not need nearly as much as I once thought I needed.

❧

"…Naked I came from my mother's
womb, and naked I will depart.
The LORD gave and the LORD has taken away;
may the name of the LORD be praised."

Job 1:21 NIV

❧

Pause to Ponder

Everything we have comes from the Lord—to include our very
life itself, our health, our house, and belongings. Everything. What
makes us think we are entitled to hang on to all of it?

Life can throw us surprises. At a time when retirement was
something to look forward to, I never expected to end up sicker
after I was home full-time. Why? It is a question we often ask. God
doesn't always give us all the answers. We take our circumstances
and do what we must with it. We learn to put our trust in God and
hope to grow from these life challenges. When life shakes us with big
challenges, we lean on God. When we feel hopeless and lost, we go
to him for help. Sometimes, we need a reminder of our source of help
and strength. When that happens, God might nudge us. We seek his
strength, his hope, his resources, his healing, and his guidance. Yes,
we ask for it all! When we are on our knees, he hears us. When our
tears freely flow, he comforts us. Even when we feel we have no place
else to turn, he invites us to knock on his door. He doesn't want us
to be timid. He wants us to knock boldly! And then, when he hears
our knock, he opens the door.

Pause for Prayer

Dear Heavenly Father,

Sometimes life can be overwhelming. Some things are just more than we can deal with all at once. Help us remember to come to you when those times come. Remind us to not try to solve all these problems by ourselves. Help us remember to pray about them and ask you to lead us to the answers. Strengthen our faith as we go through the tough times, Lord. Keep us in your Word and on our knees. Encourage us with your Word. Increase our trust in you. Thank you for holding us in your right hand during all the challenging times. Thank you for answering our knock and opening the door. Thank you for watching over us and caring about us.

In Jesus's name.
Amen.

CHAPTER 4

A Very Serious Health Nudge

I still marvel at my blessed life. I still am in awe of how God's been so good to me. Time and time again throughout my life, he's always given me everything I need. He always knows what I need and when I need it.

It had been three years since we moved back home. We had been trying to detox. We still had many residual effects of the mold. We wondered how long it would be until we felt good again. How long would it be until we had some energy? How long would it be until we had built up our immune systems, so we didn't have to be so concerned with catching illnesses? How long would it be until we could take a deep breath again and feel like we had gotten enough air? How long until the stuffy nose was no longer an issue when we were lying down? And…would our memory ever go back to what it was? Life had changed—a lot.

September came and went, and I had my annual physical. My mammogram came back with no evidence of cancer. In December, I noticed some pain when I was lying on my side. I discovered a lump in my breast. It was very deep and difficult to locate. I made an appointment to be seen. The doctor could not feel the lump as it was so deep. The technician did another mammogram and found nothing. They did an ultrasound and found nothing. I showed them where the lump was. After I showed them the location of the lump, they thought they might see a slight shadow on the ultrasound at that location.

I was scheduled for a biopsy. The biopsy was inconclusive. The panel reviewing the biopsy did not agree on the results. Some thought it was cancer. Some did not. There was only one way to know for sure.

The doctor said I needed surgery, called a lumpectomy, where they removed the lump only and a marginal area around the lump to check a larger area of tissue for cancer. I would not know if I had cancer or not until after the surgery. Anxiety set in, but it was more about the unknown. I just needed to know…was it cancer, or wasn't it?

By now, it was March. It took two weeks after the surgery for the results to come back. After two months of ongoing doctor appointments, I finally got the results. The results came back positive for cancer. It had been a long wait. My surgeon told me I was very lucky. "Your tumor was deep and very close to your chest wall," he said.

I had been doing a lot of research on cancer and cancer treatments. In the past, I had been involved in helping with care for eight family members with cancer. There was much controversy about treatment options and effectiveness. I had been doing a lot of prayer and reading the Bible for comfort and guidance. About a year before my diagnosis, I had attended a Bible study based on a book dealing with anxiety and our need to be in control. In it, there was an example of a woman going through a cancer diagnosis. I was glad I had been to that study.

Once I knew the diagnosis, there were meetings with doctors. At this point, I had already had the surgery. During the postsurgical office visits, I met with a radiation oncologist. He told me the process they go through to determine how much radiation they give people. I was amazed at the prep work that goes into the radiation treatments. As he explained the process, he smiled and said, "You might not want to eat a lot of salmon during these treatments." I knew he was trying to lighten the seriousness of the situation. I knew he wanted to reassure me of the safety of these treatments, but his humor was lost on me. It may have been a funny statement, and I am sure he meant no disrespect, but this was my life we were talking about. I had lost an acquaintance to radiation poisoning. I was not ignorant.

Next, I met with a medical oncologist. He said no IV chemo was necessary for me. What a relief it was to know that! However, he did offer me a pill. "It's just a pill," he said. While later researching, I found the pill was considered to be an oral form of chemotherapy.

I struggled with making this decision. What else should I do after the surgery to treat this? I was blessed to have a wonderful social worker for support and a wonderful oncology nurse to call at any time. My surgeon was a very kind and gentle man. I told them I needed some time to decide.

I took six weeks to make my decision. I prayed. A lot. There was so much information, and much was conflicting. There was my current state of health to consider. I truly believe each of us is different to a degree in how our body responds. I also believe we need to follow our heart to a degree, as well. In order to do that the right way, we need God's guidance to lead us to the information and help us make the right decision. It was all so overwhelming to think of making this major decision. It was like a buffet table of treatments was laid out before me, and I, the medical illiterate, was to choose what I wanted. I felt a sense of relief, finally knowing what the diagnosis was. In fact, not only was I relieved to know the diagnosis, but I actually felt at peace. I knew that peace was from God.

⁓

"Peace I leave with you; my peace I give you.
I do not give to you as the world gives.
Do not let your hearts be troubled and do not be afraid."

John 14:27 NIV

⁓

Now, I only needed God's guidance on what to do. With the surgery being done, what was next? Whenever I brought up my moldy house and fungal overgrowth situation, I felt the doctors weren't sure how to respond to that. I knew that all had a big impact on my past and current health. Because of that, I felt I had to consider that when making my decision. Going into cancer treatment when you have these other issues going on made the decisions more challenging. My immune system was clearly not functioning right, and my body was still overloaded with toxins from many sources. What would happen if I introduced even more toxins into my body during cancer treatment?

I asked God for clear and obvious guidance on what I should do.

Dear Lord, Thank you for giving me a diagnosis. I come to you with a special request. I ask that you would guide me in my treatment decisions. The choices are overwhelming. Sometimes I wish I didn't know as much as I do about these treatments.

Only you, Lord, know what my body can tolerate. Only you, Lord, know if any particular treatment will be successful. I am on information overload and need some help to make a treatment decision. Please provide me helpful information so that I can make an informed decision. Please guide me to make the best decision for me and my situation.

Because this involves so much information and is a complicated decision, please make the correct choice clear and obvious to me. I need your help Lord, as this decision is so difficult and it's an important one.

Please continue to give me peace, Lord. Please quiet the fear and give me your grace. I put my trust in you, Lord. In Jesus's name. Amen.

Although this was not easy, I found such a great sense of peace through this entire process. I was in God's Word and in prayer more than ever. I asked for his grace and his peace several times a day, every day. I was putting my trust in him to help me through this. I could clearly see his hand in so many of the things happening in my life at this time. It was very comforting to know that I was not going through this alone. I felt blessed.

I felt at peace at a time when I should have been having a harder time dealing with this. The peace was so wonderful and so welcomed after the anxiety of waiting for the diagnosis. I never would have imagined having such peace after hearing a diagnosis of cancer.

The oncology nurse explained whatever decision I made, I needed to be committed 100% to that decision and to never look back. I knew she was right.

I read inspirational literature. I surrounded myself with all things positive.

I continued to ask God to make it very obvious what I should do. He led me to so much information online and in books. I found numerous cancer support groups online. I found traditional and natural treatment groups online, as well as a community of cancer experts who were Christian. There were eating plans for people with cancer and people who had healed with natural treatments. There were also cancer researchers. The tricky part was sorting through all of those resources. Which were valid? Which were bogus? And the big question: Which would work for me, if any? There was no way to be sure. It felt like it was all a gamble. Previously I had no idea there were so many people using alternative treatments. Many of them kept it quiet.

I knew there were no guarantees to any of these treatment options, both traditional and alternative. I knew the cancer could recur. I felt in my heart that with my current medical situation, I wouldn't be able to tolerate the traditional treatment. I was in too delicate of a condition after the mold. But…I knew who was in control. It was God. The Great Physician.

The doctor's office called me several times to see if I had made a decision. They were concerned about the efficacy of radiation treatments if I waited much longer to start. I explained that I was in prayer about the situation and awaiting guidance. As I told them that, I wondered if they heard that very often. I wondered what they must be saying behind the scenes. Were they mocking me? Were they thinking I was crazy to even think of doing anything other than what they recommended?

As I prayed and worked toward a decision, I made a comparison chart with the pros and cons of various treatment options. I also listed my current health situation specifics:

- Enlarged liver. What would adding more chemicals do to my body? What would the radiation and chemo pills do to my liver?

- Compromised immune system from the mold. The immune system would be further weakened by treatments. I felt I had nothing to fight with. I was still dealing with the effects of the mold. I had candida. Would I be able to tolerate the radiation and the chemo pills? I was concerned that I would end up even sicker than I already was. I still got sick easily. If I got a cold or a sinus infection, then I would be sick for two to four months. This would mean more antibiotics, which they didn't like to give me. Once I got over the sinus infection, my doctor said it would take me two months to build up some strength again. I had trouble being healthy long enough to even get a flu shot!

As I deliberated what to do, I got an email about an online class on how to treat cancer naturally through nutrition and changing what you could with your environment to limit exposure to toxins. The instructor was a Christian. I was exposed to more knowledgeable doctors and researchers. It proved to be an encouraging and uplifting atmosphere filled with new ways of thinking and living.

More research led me to information about the psychology of cancer, the need for good sleep, relaxation, and forgiveness. There was much emphasis put on maintaining a good spiritual life, healthy eating, healthy lifestyle, exercise, and a positive mindset.

As I settled into an acceptance of my diagnosis of cancer, I also set out to implement healthy and natural ways to help fuel and restore my body on this journey. I continued praying for guidance on what I should be eating and doing.

This led to a change in what I purchased at the grocery store. I went to the local natural foods store, selected some items, and checked out. I had about twenty cans of organic beans in my cart. It was just a couple of weeks after my surgery. I still hurt physically. I was weak.

I wanted someone to carry these out to the car and load the trunk for me. At any other time I would have asked for someone to do a carryout. For some strange reason, I instead asked for someone to escort me out to my car. I don't know why I said that. No one came when the checker called for help. She called for help a second time. A man that appeared to be in his late 60s came up front. It appeared everyone else was busy.

The checkout clerk told him, "This lady would like to be escorted out to her car." There it was again…"escorted". Why had I said that, anyway? The elderly gentleman escorted me to my car. He didn't push the cart. That annoyed me. I struggled, pushing it through the slushy snow. I had recently had surgery. I had some pain. But he was no young man, and I had used a poor choice of words, so I didn't say anything. We got to my car. I opened the trunk. Surely, he would load the groceries into the trunk, wouldn't he?

He didn't put the groceries in the trunk! He just stood there talking while I put the groceries in the trunk. I found this rather odd and, again, annoying. I thought perhaps he wasn't able to lift the groceries. After all, I did ask for an escort. Maybe he thought I was worried about getting mugged!

While he watched me loading the heavy groceries into the trunk, he asked why I had bought so many cans of beans. I explained that I had just been diagnosed with cancer and I was trying to improve my diet.

He told me he was the manager of the store. I wondered why the manager was doing a carryout or escort to the car. It all seemed rather odd. He started telling me about his wife, who had been diagnosed 26 years earlier with cancer. He gave me a great deal of information about her diet, lifestyle, and a specific food supplement that she continued to take. He stood there by my car in the snow and cold in March, talking to me for 30 minutes! He was a kind, gentle man.

At the end of the conversation, he got in my personal space—you know, that distance from your face is the forbidden zone unless you know someone well. He cupped my face in his hands and looked deep into my eyes. "You can do this!" he said in an almost stern voice. I was without words at this point.

Obviously, had I requested a regular carryout, this conversation would have never happened. I would have never gotten all this good information on things to do. Was that the reason for my poor choice of words that day when I asked for someone to escort me out to my car? I do not know. I just know that I had been asking God to show me the way I should go and he was supplying a wealth of information to help guide me in the right decision for me. He was also trying to give me hope and inspiration.

Again, there was more peace. God was making an impression on me. I felt his guiding hand. I felt the comfort of knowing he was in control. He was showing me that others had fought this battle in a kinder, gentler way than doing the conventional treatment. Some of them had won the battle.

I was not confident that I could tolerate treatments. I wasn't going into this blindly. I knew there were no guarantees. I knew the cancer could come back. I prayed about that. God had been teaching me so much these past few years about trusting him. He had taught me that I shouldn't worry into the future. He didn't want me to concern myself with the what-ifs.

I started eating healthier. I started limiting my chemical and toxin exposure around the house and in my personal care products by changing many of the products we used. I had increased awareness of many things. It seemed God was leading me to a decision.

The oncology department said I needed to make my decision by no later than five or six weeks post-op. I called them and told them after much prayerful consideration, I was led to decline the radiation and the oral pills. "We are still here for you," she said. "You can still come here for your checkups and monitoring. Call us if you have any questions or concerns."

It felt strange. I was going against the conventional methods. I won't lie. It felt scary. Was I doing the right thing? I didn't know how this was going to turn out. I just needed to trust in the Lord and let him lead me.

Trust in the Lord with all your heart
And lean not on your own understanding;
In all your ways submit to him,
And he will make your paths straight.

Proverbs 3:5-6 NIV

Pause to Ponder

I would never tell anyone which treatment they should choose for cancer. Every case is different. Every person is different. What is right for one person may not be for another. Different people respond differently to the various treatments. Everyone should choose the option that is right for them, based on consultations with their personal physician. Those options are different for different people. The doctors lay out the available treatment options. Each choice must be made by the individual. No one can make that choice for them.

For me at that time, the best option was to let the Lord lead me in the direction I should go. This was partly because of my unusual circumstances due to having an already compromised immune system from living in the moldy house. It made things trickier for me. Not having any medical training background, I felt like I was in over my head trying to make this decision on my own. And so I did the only thing I could do. I turned to God.

I knew that if the cancer recurred, I would have to go through more prayer and analysis and make a decision again. Perhaps I would choose differently the next time. I didn't know.

Being diagnosed with cancer is a very humbling experience. It's definitely a nudge from God reminding you of how fragile life is and that your life is truly in his hands. It's a reminder to not take life for granted, to love others, and to ensure your relationship is right with God. It's a tap on the shoulder saying, "Make your life count for however long you have."

Pause for Prayer

Dear Heavenly Father,

Thank you for always being with us. Thank you for your peace during those turbulent moments in our lives. That priceless peace that only you can provide. Thank you for your gentle guidance when we don't know which way to go. You give us what we need to get through the challenging days on this earth. Some of life's moments require difficult decisions. Decisions that are more than we can handle on our own. Thank you for leading us to finding the answers we need to move forward. Thank you for your heavenly comfort and care.

In Jesus's name.
Amen.

CHAPTER 5

An Unusual Answer to Prayer

I had been on a quest for better health. I was trying to eat healthier, exercise, avoid chemicals, and use more natural things in my daily life. Having just had cancer surgery, I knew lifestyle changes were an important component of healing. This was not an easy road to walk.

One of the things I was supposed to be eating large quantities of was dark, leafy greens. Slowly, I introduced more and more greens to my diet. Meanwhile, I was feeling worse. I was having heart palpitations. Crazy, fast, and hard heartbeats. It was getting concerning. I started having extreme dizziness and vertigo. I was also supposed to be walking more for exercise. The dizziness was making this very difficult. I almost tipped over while walking along the side of the road. I eventually had to quit walking because it was getting dangerous. I didn't want to be lying there in the path of an oncoming vehicle. I didn't even feel safe going up and down the basement stairs.

I went to the doctor. Many times. They did an EKG. I did a cardiac stress test. They had me wear a heart monitor for a week. I did physical therapy exercises. This went on for months. They still hadn't been able to identify what was causing the severe dizziness or the crazy heartbeats. I was put on some medications. Nothing seemed to be helping.

Finally, I did what I should have done in the first place. I prayed about it. I was desperate for answers and for help. Why hadn't I done this sooner? Hadn't God been teaching me to come to him first as I had been facing these other life challenges?

Dear Lord, I come to you with a humble request. In my foolishness, I come to you after I have tried to find answers elsewhere. Forgive me for not coming to you first. These health problems are getting to be too much, Lord. I am trying to take care of myself, but things just seem to be getting worse. The doctors haven't been able to identify the problem or give me any solutions. Please reveal to me what the problem is and help me to find the solution to that problem. What is causing these crazy heartbeats and dizziness? No one seems to be able to figure it out. I ask that you would make the answer clear and obvious to me, Lord. Thank you for your love and care. I ask these things in Jesus's precious name. Amen.

One day, I had stopped at a large discount store to pick up a couple of items. I had appointments to get to and many errands to do that day. That meant that I had no time to loiter. Yet, here I was, feeling the magnetic pull. I was always drawn to the book aisle. I decided to skip it that day, as I just couldn't take the time to look at books.

As I got closer to the book aisle, I decided to take a quick stroll down it on my way to another section of the store that I needed to go to. "I won't stop. I will just speed-read titles on my way down this aisle," I told myself as I turned the cart into the book aisle. And I did. I was speed-reading titles until I got about two-thirds of the way down that aisle. Then, the unthinkable…I stopped! Oh no! Now, I would be under a time crunch. There was a title that grabbed my attention. The book was about not eating certain foods if you are taking certain medications. Well, that sounded interesting. "But, I don't have time," I thought. "I really have to get going." Yet, the intriguing title made me wonder. I could not help myself. On a whim, I picked up the book. I opened the book up to a random page spread — pages 142 and 143. Imagine my surprise when I discovered that random page just happened to be addressing **MY blood pressure medication** and **dark leafy greens**.

It said if you take my medication, you should avoid eating very much dark leafy greens. It listed the symptoms people could experience because of the conflict. It was my symptoms. It said this combination could cause irregular heartbeats and even heart attack!

> *Well, Lord, I asked you to make these answers very obvious to me and you surely did. Thank you for that information! I am in awe that you led me to this book and this page with the answer that even the doctors could not provide. My God is a mighty God! Thank you from the bottom of my heart. In Jesus's name. Amen.*

I immediately started experimenting. I reduced the dark, leafy greens. I noticed a slight difference. Then, I cut them out completely. Things were improving! I introduced more back into my diet, and it started getting worse. I had found the answer…no, wait, God had provided the answer.

Now, some might mock me and say this was merely a coincidence, but I know better than that. I had been to the doctor several times. I had undergone heart tests. I had worn a heart monitor, and the doctors were stumped. I had done physical therapy with little results. I had prayed to God, asking for clear and obvious guidance…and he had answered.

I realized I was not going to be able to do this anti-cancer diet at 100% of the recommended levels. I now knew that I was going to have to customize this diet with information I had learned and adjust it according to what my body could tolerate. This was going to take some time, observation, and work. This was going to be challenging.

It seemed so many of the things I tried to do to improve my health and hold the cancer at bay brought to light other obstacles preventing me from doing them. At times, it was a bit discouraging. It also served as a reminder to me. There was only so much I could do myself. This entire cancer walk truly was a lesson in trust. It was a walk being guided by my Heavenly Father. Regardless of which method of treatment is chosen, a cancer patient's life is truly in God's hands.

Some things that used to seem important were no longer important. What was important to me right now were faith, family, friends, and, of course, health. Materialistic things really didn't matter. I had been learning that ever since the moldy house ordeal. Had it really taken all this to get me to this point?

Through all this, I still marveled at my blessed life. I still was in awe of how God had been so good to me. He always knew what I needed and when I needed it. He's always given me everything I need—including unconventional answers to prayer. He's seen me through some things. He's used those things to grow my faith and trust in him. And now that funny feeling I get in my chest? It's not crazy heartbeats. It's my heart leaping for joy.

⚬‿⟋⟍

The LORD is my strength and my shield;
my heart trusts in him, and he helps me.
My heart leaps for joy, and with my song I praise him.

Psalm 28:7 NIV

⚬‿⟋⟍

Pause to Ponder

Coincidence? Or a nudge from God in response to prayer? What are the chances of you hurriedly going down a store aisle, noticing a particular book on the shelf…while walking quickly…and opening the book to the exact page with the answer to a medical problem you have that the doctors couldn't solve? An answer that you had been praying to God for. He truly works in amazing ways!

How many times in our lives do random things happen that make a difference for us? How many of those random events are really intentional interventions by God? How many do we recognize as being from God? When was the last time you had a "coincidence" happen? What were the circumstances?

Pause for Prayer

Dear Heavenly Father,

Forgive us for all the times we turn to everyone but you for our life solutions. Help us learn to put you first, not last, on our list of resources to draw on. Help this practice to become a habit. Thank you for all of the times you have provided us with help, both when we have asked for help and when we haven't. Your love and care amazes us. Let us never take it for granted. Help us recognize all the times you have given us help. All praise be to you!

In Jesus's name.
Amen.

More Nudged Stories

The stories in this book depict a sampling of some experiences Christians have recognized as nudges from God and how they responded to them. Although the stories are true, the author chose to change the names of the individuals and some of the locations to protect the individual's privacy. Many individuals have shared a favorite Bible passage that was meaningful to them related to their story. For that reason, you may see a few verses repeated. It demonstrates how the Word of God impacts different people.

CHAPTER 6

Peace in the Storm

They were excited. Celeste, Dave, and their three children were traveling to visit family. Those occasions we get to see relatives living a distance away are always times to be happy, and this was no exception.

Their family was young, with the children all being under ten. As they drove down Highway 14, a two-lane road, they were looking forward to their visit.

While they were traveling, storm warnings were issued. And then it started. Rain, thunder, and lightning filled the air. Between the storm and the darkness of the night, the visibility was terrible. Celeste grew fearful. Celeste was worried about tornados and the severe winds. The gusts of wind were so powerful that they made the metal on the roof of the car vibrate. A wind that strong is not something one would expect to experience during a typical storm. Being inside a vehicle on the open road during a storm like that would certainly cause unrest. Celeste had never been in such a severe storm while on the road before. All she could think about was her three young children, and she wanted to keep them safe from this storm.

A mother's love is like that. You do all you can to protect your children. You worry, you pray, and ultimately, you must give it up to the Lord to protect them. And now was one of those times. There was little else she could do.

As the storm worsened, Dave couldn't see to drive. He pulled over and parked along the side of the road. They were in the country. The rain was pummeling the vehicle. The loud blasts of thunder put fear in Celeste, and the heavenly displays of lightning looked like spider webs woven across the sky.

After sitting there for a few minutes with the fear still growing, Celeste was even more concerned about her family's safety. What if a tornado should occur? She was trying to assess if there was a ditch nearby to find refuge if a tornado did happen.

As her eyes scanned further from the side of the road, it happened. She suddenly noticed something that she hadn't seen earlier. What was that? Could it be? There it was, shining through the haze of the storm. An illuminated cross! It was not in the sky. It was not on the top of a church. It was about six to eight feet above the ground. It was not very far off the road. Celeste didn't know if there was a building there or not. If there was a building, it may have been affixed to the side of the building. It was hard to tell, as the visibility was still poor.

After seeing the cross, Celeste felt instant peace. She quit worrying about the storm and the children. She felt a great sense of comfort. How amazing it was to feel this peace and comfort during this raging storm! She knew where this comfort came from. Celeste had been nudged. The illuminated cross served as a reminder to her that no matter what is happening around us, God is with us.

They were pulled off the road for about ten to fifteen minutes. Once she noticed it, she saw the cross the rest of the time they were parked there. Soon, the storm subsided enough to allow driving, and they went safely on their way to their destination.

Celeste has traveled the same road back to that area many times since the night of that storm. Each time, she scans the countryside, looking for any kind of sign or illuminated cross there. She has never seen a cross in that location since that stormy night.

Ever since that experience, when she is afraid, Celeste remembers seeing the illuminated cross during that terrible storm. It is a reminder to her that God is in control. She often thinks about that reminder.

We may have a hard time understanding some of these things that happen in our lives. God's ways are sometimes like that. And maybe, in this life, we don't need to understand all of our experiences. Perhaps we just need to acknowledge God's presence and intervention in our lives and give thanks, even when we can't see through the storms that come in life.

We need to tell others what he has done for us. At times, when we have a special experience from God, we recognize this is something unique between us and God. He's like that. He sometimes singles us out and makes us feel special…from all the other eight billion people on this earth.

⁓

The LORD gives strength to his people;
the LORD blesses his people with peace.

Psalm 29:11 NIV

⁓

Pause to Ponder

We remember reading about a storm from biblical times. In the fourth chapter of Mark, we find the disciples were out on a boat when the waters churned heavily. Their little boat bounced around on those stormy waters, and they grew afraid. In their fear, they awakened Jesus. Jesus spoke a few words to the sea and he calmed that storm. He taught the disciples a life lesson about fear and faith.

Even in modern times, Jesus continues to calm storms. He also calms hearts. Jesus is our constant. We can always count on him to be there for us through the storms in nature and through our life storms. Sometimes God uses amazing ways to remind us that he is there, through it all, calming the storms and calming our hearts. He does this while illuminating the way through the dark and frightening times with the hope and comfort that only he can give.

It is easy for us to feel afraid at times in this life. Sometimes we forget that we can call on God in our hour of need. At times, he uses signs and wonders to give us that blessed assurance that he is there for us. Are you watching? Are you listening? Are you paying attention so that you notice his moments of comfort in your life?

Pause for Prayer

Dear Lord,

We marvel at how you care for us. You care for us physically, but you also care for our state of mind. You send comfort when we are shaking. You send reassurance when we have doubts. You send us peace when we can't find any on our own. Sometimes, things happen that make us afraid. Help us to remember to always turn to you in our fears. Give us faith and trust that you will keep your promises and take care of us. In your omnipotence, please keep us safe. And thank you, Lord. Thank you for your physical care. Thank you for those times you singled us out and made us feel special with your individualized attention. Thank you for nudging our pounding hearts to remain calm during life's frightening moments.

In Jesus's name.
Amen.

CHAPTER 7

A Young Mother's Stress

Being a young mother is a beautiful experience. It also can be very demanding and stressful. Today's mothers must be on the alert for so many challenges. They must watch social media, gaming, and internet activity. They are on the look-out for bullying, drugs, and mental illness, just to name a few. Each generation has some unique experiences to deal with while raising their children.

Emily was a young farmwife and mother during the 1950s. Young mothers then didn't have many of the challenges of raising children like we see today. That doesn't mean motherhood was any easier. Being a young mother in those days had some challenges related to the times they were living in.

Life on the farm wasn't easy. There was no indoor plumbing. The water pump was outside, and the toilet was an outhouse. Yes, that's right; the toilet was in a building outside and had no plumbing. Water for household use had to be carried from the outside pump to the house. Can you imagine having to carry water to the house for drinking, cooking, cleaning, dishwashing, bathing, and clothes washing? Now add wintery weather to this. There would be sub-zero temperatures to chill the skin and deep snow to walk on while carrying the pails. Those pails filled with water were sloshing back and forth and sometimes spilling onto the snow, ice, boots, and clothing.

When women were washing clothes, they had to heat the water in a big boiler on top of the stove. Usually, the tall boiler covered two burners and held many gallons of water. It took quite a while for the water to heat up on the stove. The washers were not as convenient as the automatic washers of today. Washing clothes was a lot of work.

Washing clothes could also be dangerous. The hot water had to be transferred into the washer tub. After washing a load of clothes, women had to retrieve the wet clothes from the washer tub and run them through the wringer. This could also be dangerous if a piece of clothing the woman was wearing or a finger or hand got wound into the wringer. Even though there were washing machines, there were still several steps and some manual labor involved. You couldn't just throw the clothes in, press a button, walk away, and return later to clean clothes.

In the winter, a bucket had to be placed under the sink to catch the drain water, as it would freeze if Emily tried to drain it to the outside of the house. Of course, the bucket had to be emptied every so often. This was especially cumbersome during the winter. When emptying the bucket, you had to be careful where you dumped it out, as it was going to create an icy patch. No one wanted to be worrying about falling down on that.

Being a young mother and farm wife posed extra challenges, as young mothers struggled to find balance in helping their husband with the farm work, maintaining the house, cooking, raising a garden, and caring for young children. Emily had a three-year-old son and a three-month-old daughter. Life was busy with farm work and two little ones in the house. The days were long and exhausting.

Much to her surprise, when Emily's youngest was three months old; she discovered she was pregnant again. She started to feel overwhelmed, wondering how she was going to do it all. How could she possibly take care of three young children so close in age? How could she keep up with all the work involved with a newborn and a one-year-old? These were the days before disposable diapers. How could she keep up with the laundry with two babies in diapers?

Anxiety set in and Emily felt it. She just wasn't sure how she could do all the farm work, house work, plus take care of three young children at a time when modern conveniences were elusive.

But God had a plan. Emily prayed. Soon Emily learned of an electric water heater that she could put in the washer to heat the wash water in the washer. Her husband took steps to try to make life easier also. He installed a pump in the basement so that she could have access to cold water in the house, instead of carrying the water in. This was especially helpful in the winter. She weaned her daughter before the baby was born.

Emily read her devotions and the Bible every day. One day, as she read her devotions contained in *Portals of Prayer*, she was led to the assurance that God wanted her to have. He led her to Philippians 4:13. That Bible verse gave her the peace that she needed. Emily knew that God was going to help her, and she no longer had to worry about how she was going to handle it all. Emily had been nudged through God's Word. Emily realized that God was in control. It was going to be alright. God was going to help her through the challenging times of motherhood. Of that, Emily was certain.

❧

I can do all this through him who gives me strength.

Philippians 4:13 NIV

❧

Pause to Ponder

We know that through our Heavenly Father we find the peace and strength we need as we face life's challenges. Although we may feel overwhelmed at times, we know that he always has our back. If we stay in his Word, we are reminded that even when we don't see the way, he has a plan and he will help us through it. Have you given your worries over to the Lord?

Pause for Prayer

Dear Father in heaven,

You always take care of us. Sometimes, we doubt. Sometimes, we stress. Sometimes, we feel so overwhelmed that we almost give up without trying. Over and over, you show us you have not forgotten us. So many times, you reveal your plans to take care of us as we face life challenges. Saying thank you doesn't feel like enough. Open our eyes to your magnificent ways of taking care of us. Keep us aware. Keep us in your Word. Remind us and nudge us so that we remember to always look to you for the solutions to all of life's challenges.

In Jesus's name.
Amen.

CHAPTER 8

The Downy Feather

It was a sunny January day. It was cold, and there was snow on the ground. It was a good day to be in the house and admire the cold wintery scene from a place of warmth.

As Ann sat in her living room with her back to the window, she heard a loud thump on the glass behind her. She wondered what that could be as she pulled back the curtain to look closer. She expected to see a kid running away after throwing a snowball at the house. Much to her surprise, there was no one in sight.

She did see something else, though. Some downy feathers were swaying back and forth as they slowly floated towards the ground. As her eyes fixed on the downward motion of the feathers, she saw it. There was the bird that had flown into the window. It was lying in the snow next to the front steps. Although she didn't know what kind of bird it was, she could tell that it was a good-sized bird, about the size of a cardinal. It was lying in the snow on the sidewalk by the door. Its head was cocked rather strangely. The elongated neck was bent out of shape, too. She was sure the bird had a broken neck.

Ann stood there for a bit, hoping that the bird was just dazed. She hoped that the bird would get up and fly away. Nothing happened. There was still no movement. She knew she couldn't just let the bird lie there on the sidewalk if it was dead. Ann hoped that the bird wasn't dead. How would this look to someone coming to her door? She turned away to wait it out, hoping it would fly away. She envisioned how she would remove the dead bird from the sidewalk. She had a mental picture of herself removing the dead bird with a shovel, with its broken neck drooping over the edge of the shovel—swinging back and forth as she carried it away.

The thought of it all made her feel sick to her stomach. Not knowing what else to do, she sat down in the chair again. She was reminded of a Bible verse.

⁂

Are not two sparrows sold for a penny?
Yet not one of them will fall to the ground
outside your Father's care.

Matthew 10:29 NIV

⁂

Surely, God knew about this bird too! She quickly prayed, "Lord, please let this bird be okay and let it fly away."

After a bit, she went back to the window and pushed the curtain back. There in the snow was the bird. It was still lying motionless.

What startled her next was the thought that went through her mind. Seeing that motionless bird was just what she expected to see! Suddenly, it struck Ann. It was a lightbulb moment. She had a rush of guilt. She sat down on the chair again and began to cry. She realized that she had a greater need for God's help than the bird lying outside.

Bible verses she had learned in her childhood came flooding back to her. They were verses about faith and prayer:

Ask and it will be given to you; seek and you will find;
knock and the door will be opened to you.
For everyone who asks receives; the one who seeks finds;
and to the one who knocks, the door will be opened.

Matthew 7:7-8 NIV

He replied, "Because you have so little faith. Truly I tell you,
if you have faith as small as a mustard seed,
you can say to this mountain,
'Move from here to there,' and it will move.
Nothing will be impossible for you."

Matthew 17:20 NIV

❧

... The prayer of a righteous person is powerful and effective.

James 5:16 NIV

❧

Ann knew she had just demonstrated that her faith could not move mountains. She was weak and had doubts. She felt she was misusing prayer. She hadn't prayed with great expectations. She thanked God for revealing her sin. She asked God for forgiveness. Recognizing this need to pray expecting that God hears our prayers and answers them brought her peace. She recognized the problem was her. She was uplifted because she remembered that God cared for her more than the sparrows.

Now she prayed with confidence and said, "Lord, I know that you are aware of my needs and the needs of that fallen bird outside. I know that you have the power to help both of us. That power is yours to use as you choose."

Suddenly, it no longer mattered to Ann about the bird. In a way, she felt she was that fallen bird. She felt that God had picked her up and revived her. She felt a burden lifted from her shoulders.

It had been about ten minutes since Ann had heard the thump on the window and seen the downy feathers floating to the ground. She got up and went to the window again. She pushed back the curtain, and there in the snow was a depression. It was the exact spot where the bird had been. Faith had stepped in. And the door had been opened. The mountain had been moved. God had just demonstrated the power of prayer.

Yes, God cared about that bird. But he cared so much more for Ann and her faith.

By itself, that downy feather couldn't do anything to help Ann. But with the Holy Spirit at work using God's Word, that downy feather had an impact on Ann and the condition of her heart.

Ann had been nudged. Nudged to remember the right use of prayer. Nudged to remember to pray with confidence knowing that God hears our prayers. And nudged to expect an answer to prayer.

~∽~

Listen to my words, LORD, consider my lament.
Hear my cry for help, my King and my God, for to you I pray.
In the morning, LORD, you hear my voice;
in the morning I lay my requests before you and wait expectantly.

Psalm 5:1-3 NIV

~∽~

Pause to Ponder

We know that God hears our prayers. We know that he has the power and means to help us. The question is, do we expect him to act? We think we believe that he can. We think we believe that he will. But do we really believe?

Going through the motions. Saying the right words in a prayer without much thought. Waiting for a quick response. How often do we do this? How often are we disappointed in the results? We know that God answers prayers in his own time, on his terms, and in ways we can't always understand. We also know that God knows our hearts. He knows us so much better than we know our own hearts. He knows when our faith needs a wake-up call. He sometimes shakes our shoulders and rouses us from our sleepy existence. One day, he roused Ann with a downy feather. He touched her heart and nudged her to a stronger faith. Has he ever roused your sleepy self? How have you been nudged?

Pause for Prayer

Dear Lord,

Please forgive us for our weakness. Please forgive our occasional lack of faith. We know you hold the power to do anything we ask of you. We know you will decide if you will give us the answers that we want to our prayers. We know each act of yours is carefully orchestrated to fulfill your plans. Please strengthen our faith. Please help rouse our sleepy hearts. Remind us of your love and faithfulness. Inspire us to live faith-filled lives for you. Lead us to pray expectantly.

In Jesus's precious name.
Amen.

CHAPTER 9

The Gift and the Blessing

Sometimes, when God nudges us, he has more in mind. Sometimes, his nudge has a domino effect. Mary knows. She experienced it.

It was a time of life when things should have been getting easier. They were settled into a different state, and they had new jobs. Their children were adults raising families of their own. Life was good.

Mary's husband, Tony, had been living with pain. Eventually, he had a hip replacement. Over time, he healed, and he was getting by. As time passed, pain became the norm as his second hip acted up more and more. He knew the time was coming for the second hip replacement.

Life would be different for quite some time. There was surgery. There was recovery time. There were weeks off of work following surgery. The weeks turned into months. Tony's job was physically demanding. It was not something he could do during his recovery time. Tony ended up being off work for six months.

His body needed rest and healing. Not working for that long meant going on temporary disability. Losing six months of income can have a devastating effect on family finances. Being less than the normal income, long-term disability income isn't always enough.

Most families need two incomes to make ends meet these days. The paychecks quit coming, but the bills didn't. The senders of the bills didn't care what a person was dealing with. When the due date came, they wanted their money.

Sometimes, life just doesn't seem fair. When a person is dealing with health problems, they often are not feeling well. They have pain. They are exhausted. They are dealing with all the emotions and stressors of health problems. If people try to rush back to work before the doctors allow it, there can be long-term consequences. It seems at a time like that, a person shouldn't have to be thinking about how to pay bills and how to buy necessary items. It just doesn't seem fair. But it was reality.

The due date for a bill was approaching, and the money wasn't there. Mary put her faith where it always had been. She knew the Lord would provide. Although she didn't know how he would supply her with the needed amount, she knew he would. And so, she prayed. She asked God to provide her with enough to pay the bill. The bill was a substantial amount. She needed $500.

One day, a friend approached her privately. "I want you to take this money," she said. "I don't want you to pay me back, just use this money for whatever you need it for." How generous and amazing that a friend would do that for Mary at such a time as this! When she looked at the amount given to her, it was $500...exactly the amount she needed to pay the bill that was coming due! God had provided for Mary and Tony. He had provided exactly what they needed when they needed it. What a relief to know that the bill would be paid!

Even though money is tight when one is going through surgery and rehabilitation, and missing work, God nudged Mary's heart through this act of Christian love. Even though she and her husband were still going through many challenges, he moved her heart to remember others who were going through difficult times. As soon as she was able to, Mary saved up the same amount that was given her, $500, and she paid it forward by giving it to someone else who was in need.

During her time of need, God nudged Mary to lean on him to provide for her. She had put her trust in God. Mary had received a gift. It was an answer to prayer. But then, God touched Mary's heart again as she eventually gave that gift to another...all because of another nudge. Yes, a nudge from God.

We sometimes hear jokes about re-gifting. Maybe re-gifting isn't such a bad thing, after all. God's Word tells us about giving. In Acts 20:35, we find, "...It is more blessed to give than to receive." Mary had been given a gift. Later, she re-gifted it and was given a blessing.

❧

And my God will meet all your needs
according to the riches of his glory in Christ Jesus.

Philippians 4:19 NIV

❧

Pause to Ponder

How often does our mighty God come to our rescue? More often than many of us may realize! Are you paying attention when these amazing events happen in your life? Do you stop to really absorb what he has done for you? And then, do you learn from it? Do you grow in faith because of it? And, the final test, does this lesson produce a response from you? That is, do you help others when you can?

When God does one of these amazing saves for you, press "Pause" and process this before you move on to dealing with the next problem in life. Oh, and don't forget to say thank you.

Pause for Prayer

Dear Lord,

We marvel at all the times you are there for us in unexpected ways. We know that we should trust you to provide our needs. Sometimes that is easier than others. When you meet our needs in such wonderful ways, you make us feel special. You reassure us that despite the challenges of life in this world, you have not forgotten us. You encourage us with your generous gifts. Thank you for those gifts. We are humbled by them. Help us to remember your loving kindness and pass it on to others as they go through life's struggles.

In Jesus's name.
Amen.

CHAPTER 10

What Does God Do With a Grandmother's Tears?

Every child is a gift from God. As Christians, we know that. But sometimes circumstances underline that fact in a way that really calls our attention to it.

Grandma Chloe was very excited as this was going to be her son's first child. She couldn't wait to hold that precious little one. They were expecting a baby boy—just what they had hoped for! It had been a perfect pregnancy. Abigail had done everything right. She had an ultrasound done at four months. The little baby boy was perfect. Excitement was building in the family as the due date drew closer.

It was July 23rd. At thirty-five weeks and three days, Abigail wasn't feeling much movement of the baby. A visit to the doctor and an ultrasound showed a small spot on the baby's lungs. This led to more visits to several different neonatologists, who eventually brought them to the neonatal unit at the University of Minnesota Hospital. A caesarian section was scheduled for the next morning in an effort to deliver the baby and assess his condition.

Lucas and Chloe drove the three-hour trip to the hospital as they felt a need to see Daniel and Abigail before the surgery the next morning. When they felt comfortable that the baby's vitals were stable and the kids were ready to rest, Lucas and Chloe left the hospital to check into their hotel room for what they hoped would be a good night of rest. Little did they know that they were about to receive a frantic call from Daniel.

Abigail was rushed into emergency surgery because the baby's heart rate had dropped dramatically. Baby Griffin was born at 11:33 PM on July 24th. By 12:15 AM on July 25th, efforts to save this precious life had ceased. The entire family was in a state of shock. They were prepared for a NICU stay but certainly not to lose this precious baby. The hospital allowed the family treasured time to cherish and hold sweet baby Griffin until later that day. Mold castings were made of his hands and feet, and Daniel and Abigail were able to give him a bath, cut a lock of his hair, and dress him in his take-home outfit. The hospital arranged for a professional photographer from the charitable organization called "Now I Lay Me Down to Sleep." The photographer was able to capture his beautiful features and the raw emotion that the family was experiencing.

Days later, the cause of Griffin's death was revealed as Hydrops, a severe and life-threatening condition caused by swelling and extra fluid in fetuses and newborns. It is almost always fatal.

The grief within the family was all-consuming. It was deep, and it was raw. Daniel made sure that their neighbors and friends knew what had happened before they went home. After all, they were expecting a family of three to be returning home. He also ensured that the beautifully decorated nursery was closed up before he brought his wife home.

After family members had gone home, they opened the nursery room door and left it set up. It was an act of faith. It was an act of expectation that God would see them through and bless them with a future child.

a second baby? This amazing image brought great comfort to the family. Could it be? Did they dare to hope? Was this baby going to become a reality after three painful losses? And who was the second baby on the ultra-sound? Who was this mysterious baby who really wasn't there? Was there some heavenly intervention going on?

The baby was born by a scheduled C-section. His name was a secret until the time came. After he was born, they revealed his name was Owen. They had originally wanted a boy. Griffin, the baby they had lost, was a boy. The two miscarriages were girls. And now...they had a boy once again.

God wasn't done reminding them of who was in charge of all things. God wasn't done reminding them that he knew of the grief they had endured and the loss that remained in their hearts. They remembered the due dates of the two boys were the same, but they were in for more surprises. When baby Owen was put on the scale in the hospital nursery, he weighed 7 lbs. 9 oz....the same weight as his brother, baby Griffin! Baby Owen was measured and found to be the same length as his brother, baby Griffin, plus ¼ inch. After they took him home, baby Owen sometimes had those inconsolable times, as all babies have. The only thing that would calm him was to lay him in the little bed in the nursery...the one that was lovingly prepared for his brother, baby Griffin.

Time went on, and grieving hearts slowly started to heal, but memories remained. The joy of Owen's presence filled some of the hollow spaces in the family's hearts. Yet, experiencing such painful loss had a lasting impact, and Grandma Chloe knew she needed to fill that void. In time, Chloe put her artistic craft talents to work. She started making memory boxes. She would deliver them to a large local hospital. She asked them to give them to parents who delivered a baby on Griffin's birthday each year. It was one way of honoring the grandson she would never know in this life.

Grandma Chloe still has random thoughts of Griffin. She looks at the tree that they planted in his memory. She sees how much it has grown. It is a reminder to how much Griffin would have grown if he were still with them.

God wasn't done working on her yet. Through all the hurt, all the grief, and all the loss, he had been preparing her for a greater mission. God was nudging her. He touched her heart. He reminded her of how much love she had to give. He reminded her of how upset she used to get at the parents she dealt with in her cases at work. Those parents didn't properly care for and love their children. He moved her. He nudged her to do something to help others. He nudged her to be an advocate for children who can't speak for themselves. What do you do with a heart full of love that is left after the tears? You serve others.

Soon, Chloe became involved with a court-appointed child advocacy group. She did volunteer work by being an advocate for children who had been removed from their homes due to neglect or abuse and placed in foster care. She had the perfect background from her previous full-time work in social services prior to retirement. She also had a heart for children. She visits the homes of children in foster care, daycares, and schools. She also participates in supervised parent visits. She does this on a weekly basis and reports to and coordinates with lawyers and the courts on the situation. She became the one constant figure in the children's lives.

Chloe wants to pay it forward. She wants to fill the void by honoring the grandson she lost through honoring and loving other children. Being a substitute education assistant in pre-school and elementary schools in her hometown has allowed Chloe to continue interacting with and loving children in her retirement.

Losing grandchildren and seeing your adult child grieve deeply is painful. Experiencing grief and loss can bring us to our knees. Every fiber of our being is affected. It takes effort to overcome. Yet faith can help. God is there if we let him console us and lift us up. He sees our tossing and turning at night. He knows of the tears we shed. And he uses all the pain, all the loss, and all the grief to support his greater plan. We may not know what that plan is at the time. We may never know, but when we feel that tug on our heartstrings, when that certain Bible verse speaks to us, when we experience that call to serve others, that is a nudge. That nudge from God cannot be denied. And when you respond to the nudge, you will be blessed.

❧

You keep a record of my tossing and turning.
Keep my tears in your bottle.
Aren't they all listed in your book?

Psalm 56:8 EHV

❧

Pause to Ponder

What does God do with a bottle full of our tears? Sometimes, God uses some of the most painful moments of our lives to move us. Sometimes, deep, painful, aching grief is one of those moments. A season where our life stands still while the world continues around us. It is a season in our life where we not only ache and grieve ourselves, but we also grieve for those we love most who are experiencing heart-wrenching grief. And sometimes, watching others grieve to the core of their being is almost too much for us to bear. Yet, if we are watching, and if we are listening, and if we really pay attention to what is happening around us, we may find a new purpose in our lives. We may find joy again and all because God moved us. Once again, he is at work in our hearts using circumstances, yes, even grief, to bring good things from the bad. It is all part of his plan. It is all part of his purpose for us. Our reason for being.

Perhaps those heart-wrenching circumstances led you to serve him with a new purpose: to fill a need that only you can fill in the way that you can fulfill it. All because you looked past the grief. You set that aside and let that still, small voice in your heart follow God. Yes, you were nudged by God. Nudged to take that grief, use that pain, and turn it into something positive by serving others.

What does God do with a bottle full of tears and a heart full of love? You would be amazed! Slowly, peace and joy find their way back to you. In return, God gives you a happy heart. After a period of grieving, it feels good to have a happy heart.

Pause for Prayer

Dear Lord,

Grief is hard. We struggle with it often. We get angry. We ache. We cry. It is one of the biggest challenges we face on Earth. When we struggle to get our lives back in those times, be with us. Help us to remember you care. Help us to remember you offer us comfort in our grief. Help us to remember that every night we spend tossing and turning and every tear we shed does not go unnoticed by you. Remind us of what the future holds for believers. Let the knowledge of the coming reunion in heaven lift our spirits. Heal our grieving hearts, Lord. Use that grief in a way to make us better. Use that grief in a way to honor you. Give us strength and comfort when we struggle with grief. Help us to find joy and purpose again.

In Jesus's name.
Amen.

CHAPTER 11

Awaiting Heaven

Norah's mother was a devout Christian. She had a faith unlike most. Norah credits her grandmother's strong faith in God for infusing her mother with a drive to save souls for the Lord. This strong faith helped her mother, Evelyn, and her grandmother, Elizabeth through many difficult trials in life.

Evelyn loved her garden and kept one well into her advanced years. She played the organ at home and loved the old familiar hymns of years ago. She didn't care much about changing or updating the traditional hymns or church service to newer styles. She wasn't afraid to express her opinions on the matter, either.

Evelyn had two daughters. Norah, the youngest, was a free spirit who loved all animals. As a nurse, she also cared for people throughout her career. Norah had given her mother some challenges throughout her life. Eventually, the effects of aging set in on Evelyn and took its toll on her for the last few years of her life. Despite the veil of dementia coming over Evelyn, there were certain things she remembered. She did not know the names of her daughters or granddaughter anymore, but she could describe them. Her oldest daughter, Jane, she described as loving. She referred to her granddaughter as being common sense. Then there was her youngest daughter, Norah. One day, Norah asked her mother to describe Norah, knowing that her mother didn't realize who she was talking to. "Naughty," said Evelyn, "Very naughty!" Norah felt her mother thought of her as a rebel, and even in these sunset days of Evelyn's life, she still remembered the challenges her youngest daughter had given her over the years. Being older and wiser, Norah recognized the challenges she had presented to her mother, and she loved her mother dearly.

Evelyn's faith was strong, and it made a lasting impression on people. She loved to talk about her Savior and wanted very much to save souls for the kingdom. It was a great comfort to Evelyn's daughters to know of their mother's strong faith as she grew older and more frail.

The advancing years took their toll on Evelyn. By the time she was in her nineties, Evelyn's spine had curved dramatically, and she became very hunched over, facing forward, head pointing towards the floor at almost a 45-degree angle. She would have to lift her head and turn it to be able to see people and make eye contact with them. It looked very uncomfortable. Eventually, she had to go to a nursing home.

With Evelyn's daughters being nurses, they both knew what to watch for. In time, they recognized that Evelyn would not remain here for much longer.

As the end of Evelyn's life on this earth drew near, her daughters sat with her, each holding one of Evelyn's hands. They provided Evelyn with the comfort of some hymns. As one of Evelyn's favorite hymns started playing, Norah and Jane started singing along to "In the Garden". Evelyn loved being in her garden. She had often said she felt closer to God when she was in the garden. What a comfort hearing this song must have been to Evelyn at this time!

As her girls held their mother's hands, they had no idea that they were about to witness something amazing. Suddenly, Evelyn opened her eyes and sat up straight in bed! The years-long constraints of a bent backbone had been lifted from her. This was incredible to witness. But that wasn't all. She had a soft glow and the most peaceful expression on her face. She was looking forward and looking very happy. It was obvious she saw someone who was meeting her to take her on her journey. Norah and Jane were in awe and very touched by what was happening. Norah described it as being the most beautiful thing she had ever seen and experienced in her life. The memory of that beautiful glow around her mother stands out in her memories.

⌘

Those who look to him are radiant;
their faces are never covered with shame.

Psalm 34:5

⌘

After several minutes, Evelyn's soul separated from her body as she slumped back to the bed. Norah and Jane knew they had seen something from God. "We've seen a miracle," Jane said to Norah.

Evelyn's daughters felt blessed that they had been able to be with Evelyn and witness what they did. Norah felt that Evelyn and God wanted to ensure that she believed in God. Norah also felt that Evelyn wanted to ensure that she believed what Evelyn had taught her about God was true.

Although Evelyn had just passed away, she was not done giving her personal testimony for the Lord yet. Evelyn had planned her own funeral. Several days later, the funeral service was conducted. Much to the surprise of most of the attendees, Evelyn used her funeral to give a final testimony of her faith. As the funeral service was about to end, the pastor told the attendees that Evelyn had recorded herself singing "What a Friend We Have in Jesus." She wanted it to be played at her funeral. The tape included a few brief comments from Evelyn. Tears flowed freely that day as family and friends mourned an earthly loss, but they also were touched by Evelyn's beautiful final testimony as they celebrated another soul in heaven.

And Evelyn didn't need to worry. Her rebel-daughter received the message. She takes every opportunity she gets to share with others what she witnessed that day and the impact it has had on her faith today. She feels called to reach out and tell people about God. She wants to continue her mother's legacy to help with saving souls for Jesus.

In that moment of having to let go of her mother, Norah saw that death isn't about sadness and loss as much as it is about the joy of stepping into God's presence for all of eternity. Norah knew that for her mother, death didn't win. Death wasn't the end. Norah knew that by living for God, she would someday be reunited with her mother again. This time, it would be forever. That would indeed be something to celebrate. Yes, all of those things help take the sting out of death.

Where, O death, is your victory?
Where, O death, is your sting?

1 Corinthians 15:55 NIV

Pause to Ponder

The life we lead can impact many people. We can be responsible for shining our light and, by example, showing others the path to God. People are watching. What do they see when they look at us?

Are they encouraged and growing in faith? When they look at us, do they see a life to model? When we depart this life, what will they remember about us? Will they remember someone who lived their life for the Lord?

Pause for Prayer

Dear Lord,

Help us to live our lives for you. Help us to be an encouraging example to others. People are watching us. We influence many without our being aware of it. Let it be the kind of influence you would like us to be. Help us to make a positive difference in this world. When we leave this shell of a body, let others remember the reflection of you that they saw in us. We are not perfect, but with your help, we can make a difference and help others in their faith. Lead us in the way we should go. When our work here is done, please bring us home to you in heaven.

In Jesus's name.
Amen.

CHAPTER 12

Autumn Ministry

As we go through life, there are changes. Changes in priorities. Changes in interests and hobbies. Aging may limit us. We may gain or lose a spouse. Our health may change. No matter the changes, God is still working on us. He still calls us to do his work for him.

Rose was a very busy senior citizen. She was young at heart and very active in the community. She was always smiling, laughing, and cheerful. She had things to do and places to go. She was in no way ready to slow down...not yet anyway!

But God is the one in control, and he had other plans. One day, Rose was in a bad car accident. She was in a great deal of pain. A week and a half after the accident, Rose had an MRI to check for the source of her pain. She learned that to improve her quality of life, she had to make a choice. The choice was to do nothing and stay status quo or subject herself to surgery in an attempt for improvement.

The accident had injured her spine. The doctors carefully laid out her options. She was offered lumbar spinal surgery. No surgery is without risk, and the doctors made sure that Rose was aware of the risks of this surgery. A successful surgery could mean the end of the pain; however, this surgery is unsuccessful for five percent of the patients undergoing it.

That is a frightening thing to face. Rose felt she had no choice but to do the surgery, so she decided to go ahead with it. Even though there was risk involved, the odds were in her favor. Unfortunately, it turned out that Rose was one of the statistics. She was in that five percent. Her legs became numb, and they just couldn't hold her up. Rose ended up in a wheelchair. There were long and hard sessions of physical therapy. She felt she was almost ready to walk when her insurance stopped paying for the therapy. How disappointing this must have been. She had been hopeful for a successful surgery and recovery, and now, as she was struggling to regain mobility, she was denied treatment. She tried everything she could think of to get her insurance to reverse their decision, but all of her attempts failed.

When times were discouraging, when her body gave out, when the insurance refused to make any more payments for therapy, when things looked bleak, what did she do? Rose prayed. "I could not survive without my faith," she says.

Clearly, things were changing for Rose. There were more choices to be made. Because of the physical limitations she was facing, Rose felt there was no other choice. She had to move into assisted living. She needed help getting in and out of bed and doing other physical tasks. It would have been easy for such an active, giving person to get a bad outlook on life. Although this major lifestyle change involved all things physical, it also required an adjustment of the mental type, as well.

Rose has many talents and gifts that don't require the ability to walk. She is a gifted seamstress and makes beautiful quilts and wall hangings.

She has a love for the Lord. Prior to the accident, Rose had studied pastoral care. Two of the local major hospitals worked together to provide the training. She used her pastoral care training as a hospice volunteer for 12 years. She specialized in offering comfort to the dying who were alone.

One day prior to her accident, Rose went to visit a hospice patient for the first time. Some might feel helpless and useless as they visit someone on the brink of death, especially someone who was a stranger to them. But Rose was prepared. She had training. Rose also knew of her calling from the Lord to provide comfort and hope to the dying. As Rose walked in, she learned the lady was already in a coma. Rose sat down beside her. She sang hymns to her. After an hour or two, she started singing "Just as I Am" to the comatose lady, this stranger, who was getting close to death. Suddenly, the lady sat up and smiled. Then, just as quickly, she lay down and died. To be able to give such a gift to the dying is truly a blessing to both the dying and the giver.

But now, Rose's formerly active life faced some dramatic changes. She could have chosen to be bitter. She could have chosen to have a bad attitude. But God was providing comfort and guidance. She knew her life was changing. She looks at this as an opportunity to do the Lord's work in a new setting. She feels it is part of God's plan for her to help spread the gospel at the assisted living facility. She also feels it is part of her mission to help give peace to those dying at the facility where she lives.

Rose is an advocate for the Bible class held in the assisted living facility by trying to bring others to hear God's Word. At such a time in life, many who live there struggle with discouragement. Besides their physical bodies wearing out, some of them are living with dementia. Imagine trying to follow along in Bible class when dealing with dementia. Some persons can vary widely in their mental state from day to day and moment to moment. One day, they may come into Bible class smiling and in tune with what is happening. Another day, that same person may come into class and look like a different person. The smile is replaced with a stressed look and a frown. Confusion abounds. What was an easy task in the last class now becomes a struggle. Those who are mentally sharp help find the right page and point to the right place on a printed sheet of Bible verses. Embarrassment may give way to apologies. It is then that the loving compassion of the class members and the Bible study leader help to console them. Practicing that compassion and giving that consolation is a gift. Surely, God has strategically placed supportive and encouraging people there as part of his plan to help others through the aging process.

How does Rose know she should be doing this work for the Lord? She has been nudged. She listens to and follows God's nudges in her life. She reads the Word of God in the Bible and attends Bible classes. As she studies God's Word, she knows when he is nudging her. She listens to her shepherd. She follows where he leads her. Through a car accident, God led her to carry on her work for him in a different setting. In the autumn of her life and during one of the biggest struggles of her life, God still had important work for her.

At a time when it would be easy to be discouraged and lose hope, Rose kept her eyes on God. Despite her physical limitations and despite the constant pain, she knew that God looked at her and saw a faithful servant he still could use. She knew he didn't want her to dwell on all the challenges in her life. He had more work for her to do. Throughout her life, he had prepared her for this important work. Rose was ready. It was time to roll up her sleeves and get back to work. Same work. New location.

We have different gifts, according to the grace given
to each of us. If your gift is prophesying,
then prophesy in accordance with your faith;
if it is serving, then serve;
if it is teaching, then teach;
if it is to encourage, then give encouragement;
if it is giving, then give generously;
if it is to lead, do it diligently;
if it is to show mercy, do it cheerfully.

Romans 12:6-8 NIV

Pause to Ponder

Life sometimes sends us challenges. It is easy to become absorbed in them. We all have strengths and talents given to us as a gift from God. Throughout our lives, we gain experiences which prepare us for future assignments. Even as we grow old and our bodies deteriorate, God sees us as valuable. Looking beyond the challenges, we know that God wants us to use our gifts to help others.

Pause for Prayer

Dear Lord,

Sometimes we lose our focus. It is good that you remind us of the challenges others face, even as they continue to serve you and others. Thank you for giving us those reality checks. Be with those who are dealing with major life changes. Encourage them. Surround them with your love and protection. Comfort and provide relief for those who struggle with pain. Keep us mindful of them in our prayers and visits. Just as they serve others despite their limitations, let us be nudged to serve others as well. Thank you for the blessings you provide to them and for the blessings they provide to us.

In Jesus's name.
Amen.

CHAPTER 13

The Long Road to Faith

Sometimes life is hard. Some people have to endure far more than the average person. Although it may not seem fair, life in a sin-filled world can be hard. Someone's life may look good to an outsider who has no idea what that individual may have silently endured for most of their life. But one thing we know for certain. God has a plan, and he will use it for his good. We are a product of not only our beliefs but also what has happened to us. Life events shape us. All that while, through the trials and tribulations, God is there as he carries us through those difficult times. Unfortunately, we may not always know that.

That's how it was with Gale. She was a cute little five-year-old, fair-haired and chubby-cheeked. It was Sunday morning. Her mother was struggling with her to put on a red sweater shirt and a blue plaid skirt for church. The outfit was so cute, but Gale wanted no part of it—not anymore. Gale felt so sad and upset. What her mother didn't know was that when Gale, at five years old, had last been wearing that cute outfit, she was molested by a relative. Gale hated that outfit because of what had happened when she was wearing it. Her mother kept trying to get Gale to wear red, and Gale resisted. Her mother told others, "She's so picky about her clothes."

That same year, Gale's family moved a short distance away. By the time Gale was in second grade, she was struggling a bit in school. Gale's teacher told her mother she needed help at home with math flashcards and spelling. But there was no help from her mother. Eventually, a family friend, who was a teacher, started helping Gale with the flashcards and spelling. Still, the struggles in school continued. The teacher told Gale's mother that Gale might have to repeat the second grade. The teacher did tell Gale's mom that if she worked with her over the summer, perhaps third grade would work out okay for her. Sadly, Gale's mother made the decision to not even try and asked to have Gale held back to repeat second grade. Gale's friends went on without her, and she remained behind without any familiar friends. Gale felt betrayed by her mother.

Gale was always confused. Gale was made to feel dumb and stupid. She would go into the woods to talk to God. She knew God, but she was always seeking God. She loved basking in God's creation in the great outdoors. She enjoyed living on the farm and spending time in the barn with her Dad. It was a pleasant reprieve from time spent with her mom in the house. Once Gale was back in the house, her mom would ask her, "What is wrong with you?" or "Why don't you understand anything?" These statements would echo in Gale's head for years.

Despite the rough beginnings, God was watching out for Gale. Her grandmother and great-grandmother played a much more nurturing and motherly role than her mother did. She called them Big Grandma and Little Grandma. Gale and her sister would spend weekends with Big Grandma and Little Grandma.

Gale's dad had a business along with his farming. He liked to give his fellow farmers a break, but soon, he was taken advantage of. Unfortunately, many of his patrons didn't pay for their goods and services. About that time, Gale's mom went on vacation by herself to California. When she came back, she started saying they should move to California. All of Gale's aunts and uncles on her dad's side were living there. She also hoped Gale's dad would stop drinking if he moved to California. Her mom had a habit of badgering people until she got her way, and this was no exception. Eventually, the family moved to California.

Here was another move for a young girl already feeling very vulnerable. Her world was about to be turned upside down.

Gale's dad left first for California, while Gale, her sister, and her mom stayed at Big Grandma's. Gale's mom did her own thing. Fortunately, Big Grandma and Little Grandma were there for Gale and her sister.

Gale's dad found a job working at a huge farm and eventually sent for Gale, her sister, and her mother. When Gale was eleven years old, she visited the farm where her dad worked. He told her there were rules on the farm. Gale loved animals and said she wanted to see the animals. Her dad told a co-worker to take her to see the kittens. That proved to be a bad experience. The hired hand molested her three times over the next year. She never told anyone, but she did warn her younger sister to stay away from that man as he'd do bad things to her. At such a young age, Gale was already learning that we need to empower ourselves with God and that parents should be teaching their children how to protect themselves.

The following year, the family moved again. This time to Fresno. Gale was now twelve years old and at a very vulnerable age. Gale was experiencing culture shock. She had moved from the Midwest, where only Caucasians and Native Americans lived in her area. Now, she was being exposed to a wide variety of ethnicities. It was a mix of many cultures, and the young farm girl from the Midwest was not prepared for the viciousness she was about to encounter.

California's clothing trends were ahead of Wisconsin's. Gale was outfitted in polyester clothes. The California kids were wearing denim jeans. The bullying started. Gale was picked on about her out-of-style clothes. She had already been labeled dumb by her mom. Now, she was also labeled as a dork at school. Her parents didn't have a lot of money to buy clothes. She told her mom about the bullying, but true to her character, her mom didn't do anything. She didn't believe Gale. She felt Gale wasn't being truthful.

Eventually, Gale was bussed to another school seven miles away from her younger sister. This school was in a rough neighborhood. Gale was shocked to learn that she was one of only two Caucasian children in her fifth-grade class. She walked into class that first day to an unheard of welcome. "Look at her!" they were saying in between their bursts of laughter. She was wearing a green dress and knee socks. It's strange how much detail one can remember of traumatic incidents.

Gale was always late to class because of the unusual school bussing program in California. Arriving late left Gale feeling like she entered class with a spotlight shining on her. It provided all the more fuel for the bullies to call attention to Gale's clothing—clothing that was perfectly fine, but not like theirs.

Gale was finding it very difficult to focus on learning while she was being relentlessly bullied. Her classmates picked on her and pulled her hair. They had their ways of letting her know how they felt about her. One day, they left a paper sack on her desk. Inside it, she found a rotten orange with a note. The note read, "You are goofy." Some of her classmates were making threats about beating Gale up. As a result, she became afraid to go to the bathroom.

In Spanish, they would say, "There goes Whitey." Yes, she was experiencing that ugly word…discrimination. The only other Caucasian girl in her class had been in the school district since kindergarten. The other girl hung back, like a wallflower, and stayed silent, so they left her alone.

Being a year older than most of her classmates, Gale was more well-developed than her classmates. The boys would pick on her because of that, as well. They would grab at her breasts. The formative years for young girls can be challenging and very sensitive. In addition to that, there was a lack of support from her mother. It was beginning to be too much for a young girl to bear.

One day, during recess time, the girls formed a circle around Gale. One of the girls started calling Gale names and hit her. Suddenly, one of the girls started beating on her while the others were pulling on her hair. They got scared when she fell to the ground and started crying for help. They all left.

Gale immediately went to the principal's office. He sent her to the nurse's office and called Gale's mom at work. Gale's mom told him she couldn't leave work to come and get her. So Gale waited in the principal's office until it was time to go home. Then she rode her usual two buses home from school. When she got home, her mom wasn't home from work yet, so her younger sister, Marsha, took care of her. Marsha combed out Gale's hair. The hair that had been pulled on by the mean girls on the playground.

When Gale's mother got home from work, they discussed the incident at school. Gale's mother wondered what had brought that on. She still was not attuned to the pain and agony her daughter had been experiencing the entire time at school.

Gale continued trying to talk to her mother about all the difficulties at school. Her mother just couldn't grasp it. Her mother was different. Her mother was mostly concentrating on herself. Nothing clicked. As a result, Gale's mom asked Gale what she did wrong to the girls that they wanted to beat her up.

Over time, the school kids quit fighting. Physically, that is. The bullying, however, continued. So did the name-calling. Not surprisingly, Gale's academics suffered.

Meanwhile, Marsha had made a new friend. Marsha's new friend invited Marsha and Gale over to her house. They loved going over there to play and visit. They felt good about themselves when they were there. They felt safe and secure. Marsha's friend's mom, Sylvia, became a surrogate mom for them.

Summer brought some relief. They spent as much time as possible at Sylvia's house. It was an enjoyable summer. It was a much-needed break from the stress of what had been going on at school. Sylvia knew there were problems at home with Gale and Marsha's mom. She was helping them out. Going there was like a sanctuary for them. They could be comfortable. Sylvia took them shopping. Gale's mom gave them money so they could update their wardrobes in hopes that they wouldn't be picked on so much. Gale and Marsha were gone a lot that summer. As long as they did their chores, their mom didn't mind their being gone.

During this time in her life, Gale always went to church with her parents. They never missed church. Gale's mom had faith, but she couldn't grasp having a personal relationship with God. Meanwhile, Gale and Marsha continued to go to Sylvia's house. Their surrogate mother, Sylvia, told Gale, "God is your mother too. Your mother, your father, your everything!" Gale felt she had many special mothers in her life during these trials.

Although the family was physically altogether, Gale felt very much lacking in family support and love from her mother emotionally. There was a feeling of disconnection, absence, and rejection of her mother. Abandonment, yes that was it. Abandonment.

Gale had attended one school from kindergarten through fourth grade in Wisconsin. By the time she entered fifth grade, Gale had moved to California. She attended remedial classes during her fifth, sixth, and seventh grades. In sixth grade, it was labeled "The Reject Class". She had an encouraging teacher. This helped immensely after being picked on relentlessly for the past year in a poor learning environment.

When Gale went on to sixth grade, she went to middle school. She was actually looking forward to it. It would be a pleasant change after dealing with all the mean girls from fifth grade. Imagine Gale's surprise when she encountered those girls again, as she learned they were being bussed to her current school! Gale became good friends with a Black girl named Cassandra. Cassandra told Gale that she had to learn to stick up for herself if she was going to be able to survive this brutal environment. She told Gale the only way she was going to be accepted or left alone was to fight these troublesome girls at her school. That day soon came.

Cassandra was from a poor family and she was street smart. As the bullying increased, Cassandra recruited her brothers and sisters to host a practice fight lesson to give Gale some experience. They showed her different moves on how to fight. That practice fight came just in time. Gale was in two fights in sixth grade.

One day, while in sixth grade, Gale was sitting on the top of the circular monkey bars. A boy grabbed her leg and pulled her down. Gale hit the rungs on the way down and got hurt. Gale was taken to the nurse's office. The principal called Gale's mother at work. Her mother said she couldn't come to get her. Gale rode the bus home from school. When her mother got home from work, she had a question for Gale. She wanted to know what Gale had done to make the boy do that to her.

In sixth and seventh grades, Gale experienced many confrontations that led to fights. There seemed to be no end to the fighting. By the time Gale was in seventh grade, she was tired of it. She was getting mean. She started acting like a tomboy. She was getting tougher. Since no one else was looking after her, she was going into survival mode.

By this time, Gale was starting to encounter even more serious fights. There were cliquish groups in seventh grade, and things were getting vicious. One day, Gale's friend, Cassandra, organized a fight in the bathroom. Gale knew about the fight. Cassandra said Gale needed to prove herself to the clique so that they would understand she wasn't going to be bullied anymore.

As Gale walked into the bathroom, she was stunned to see the entire room was packed with girls. They were sitting on the towel holders, in the sinks, and anyplace they could fit.

Gale was instantly scared. She cried out to God inside her mind. "I'm going to die. Help me, God! There's no way out!" One of the girls wore large rings on every finger. The rings were covered with rhinestones. Rhinestones in settings with jagged edges. As one of the girls approached Gale while displaying her ring-covered fingers, others covered the bathroom door. There was to be no escaping.

To start the fight, someone pushed Gale into the girl wearing the rings. Gale's friend, Cassandra, said, "Go for the face! Don't stop! Go!" Another girl pushed Gale. She said, "Fight! Fight! Fight!" Gale released the long pent-up anger and fear. Gale beat up her opponent. The girl was screaming for help. Gale had girls on her back, hitting her and pulling her hair. Suddenly, Gale felt someone in the group grab her by the arm and yank her out of the bathroom. It was her defender and fight coach, Cassandra. Gale hit the wall hard and scratched up her face. The other girls took off and ran to their classes.

Gale and Cassandra went to the Principal's office. He called Gale's mom. As usual, her mom said she couldn't come until after work. Gale had to ride the bus home after school. Once again, her younger sister played nursemaid for her. When her mother came home from work, she said, "What did you do, Gale?" That's how it always was. She always assumed Gale had done wrong. That Gale had started the trouble.

Gale was suspended from school for three days after the fight. This was all disturbing to Gale's dad. He went to the principal's office. He was upset. He wanted to know why Gale had been suspended instead of the other girls. The principal told him that he would rather have one set of parents angry at him than seventeen sets of parents. The only good thing about Gale's three-day suspension was it provided her some brief protection from the mean students.

After she returned from the three-day suspension, no one bothered Gale anymore. But after all she had been through, Gale became rebellious. She needed a way to numb the pain. She was exposed to drugs in eighth grade. She would sometimes drink also, just to feel numb. Despite the horrific challenges at school, she always looked forward to the summertime. She continued to go with her sister to Sylvia's place in the mountains for the weekends, where she enjoyed some peaceful time with nature.

Ninth grade proved to be a pivotal year for Gale. She was searching. She was exploring the good girl versus the bad girl. During this time, Gale had two very influential friends. One was a good Christian girl, and one was a bad influence, leading her down the path of taking drugs and drinking. Gale went back and forth, spending a day with one friend and then the next day with the other friend while exploring different lifestyles. She wanted to be good, but she had more fun being bad by doing drugs and drinking. Things were spiraling out of control during her freshman year. Gale was heavy into doing pot. She was drinking and cutting school to get high. As if this wasn't enough, she continued to be influenced by this bad girl who came from a messed up family. During this time, she was also trying to find Christ in between all of that.

Gale became numb to escape the reality of the life she was trapped in. One day, Gale, her girlfriend, and her friend's boyfriend skipped school. Another boy came along with them. As the day went on, Gale eventually excused herself to go to the bathroom. He was waiting for her when she came out of the bathroom. And then the unthinkable. He raped Gale. Depression set in. Gale didn't care anymore. Life had become unbearable. As life became more and more intolerable, despair took over. Gale just wanted to kill herself.

Gale's mom talked to relatives about her. She led them to believe that she was a bad person. She also tried to get various relatives in California to let Gale stay with them. They all declined.

After her freshman year of high school, Gale came back to Wisconsin for a visit with her grandma over the summer. Her California friends wrote to her that one of her male friends, Tim, had been stabbed that summer. Meanwhile, in Wisconsin, Gale had her first summer love with a boy named Ryan. She knew Ryan previously. They bonded over coming from homes with dysfunctional moms. They formed a close relationship. Things were good that summer. She wanted to stay in Wisconsin to escape all the negative things happening in California and because she now had a boyfriend in Wisconsin. Much to her dismay, her mom would not let her stay in Wisconsin after the summer vacation ended.

Gale went back to California for her sophomore year of high school. Gale's mom had taken her to professional counselors in sixth grade and again during her sophomore year of school. Both times, Gale's mom was told that there was nothing wrong with Gale. Gale was perfectly normal. The counselor told Gale's mom that she was the one that needed counseling. And yet, the denial continued. In her mom's eyes, everything was Gale's fault.

Gale's dad was gone to work all week until Friday night or Saturday mornings. When he was home on the weekends, he worked at another job, so he wasn't around home very much. Gale wasn't rebellious when her dad was around. She felt she could trust him.

The one positive thing Gale had to hang onto was her summer love back in the Midwest. Ryan was one of the good things in her life. They started calling each other and talking…a lot. Unknown to the new boyfriend, his mom called up Gale's mom. "The relationship is over," she stated. She didn't like all the long-distance calls, and she said that they were too young. So there it was. One of the few good things in her life was taken from her. The one thing that made her happy and gave her hope. By now, Gale didn't care.

Meanwhile, Gale started dating Tim, the young man who had been stabbed. Things quickly deteriorated. They were both drinking and smoking pot. Gale liked getting high and being numb. Gale was out of it. In time, she couldn't bear another day of it. A couple of years later, when she reached her lowest point, she acted. She reached for her bottle of prescription tranquilizers and tried to take her life. She was trying to cover up the pain with the drinking and the drugs. She felt like she was in a dark valley. She was calling out to God and searching.

❧

Even though I walk through the darkest valley,
I will fear no evil, for you are with me;
your rod and your staff, they comfort me.

Psalm 23:4 NIV

❧

Things were getting out of control. Gale didn't know it, but God had a plan. He always does. She was working her way back to God. She went to several churches. They served as wake-up calls. Things were slowly progressing. Every encounter was drawing her closer to God. She was having times where she would talk with someone of faith and she would have a special moment. It was at those times she would think, "I want this."

Despite the progression towards a relationship with God, the home life wasn't getting any better. Tim was physically and verbally abusive. He wouldn't get a job. He took her money and bought drugs with it. Life for Gale became a cycle of: work, go home, drink, do drugs, argue and fight, go to bed, get up, and go to work again. Day after day, the hopeless cycle continued. All this time, Gale kept a picture of Ryan, her summer love from the past, who was back in Wisconsin. There was no contact between them.

Gale was working at a large chain discount store. She was fortunate to be surrounded by many friends. The stress and abuse had changed her physically and mentally. She had gone from a size 8 to a size 16. An old friend came into the store one day. He looked shocked and said, "What happened to you, Gale? Are you still with Tim?" "Yes," she replied. This made her think. She went home from work and looked in the mirror. "You don't look like Gale," she told herself. And then came the revelation, "I'm not me anymore!"

It was July 13, 1985. Gale stayed up stoned for three days watching the Live Aid Concert. In pain, she cried out to God. "Are you real? Is this life?" She hated the way she felt. The drugs and the drinking… they just weren't helping anymore. The pain was too sharp and could not be dulled. Despite all this pain, and unknown to Gale, God was setting the stage.

After three days off, she returned from her stoned weekend watching the Live Aid concert on TV. A friend asked Gale to go to a crusade. She had asked her over and over in the past. And today, she was asking Gale again. Gale responded, "If I go with you once, will you quit bugging me?" "Yes!" she said. On July 18, 1985, the women attended a crusade. The crusade was a Christian revival event. It was a day Gale would never forget. It was the day she accepted Jesus Christ. The topic of the crusade was "What Junk Do You Have In Your Carpetbag?" "Drinking and drugs," Gale thought to herself. "I am sick of carrying this around." At the crusade, they did an altar call. Gale went forward and accepted the Lord. As she stood there, she felt a hand on her. She turned around to see that a man had placed his hand on her. She wanted to lash out at him, but suddenly, she felt a peace come over her. This man from the crowd who had placed his hand on her was praying for her!

Finally, Gale felt seen by God. She also felt she had seen God. She never felt her mother saw her. Between her mother and her husband, she had felt overlooked, unloved, and trampled on for all these years…but now, it was different. She knew that God saw her pain, the abuse she had endured, the abandonment she felt, and her feelings of hopelessness and helplessness. He also saw her weaknesses. He saw it all, and he loved her. He claimed her as his own. How good it felt to be seen and loved!

From that point on, Gale gave up all alcohol, drugs, and cigarettes. She did it immediately. No tapering off. No crutches. Instantly and completely. She didn't feel any cravings or after-effects! This was significant. However, she was still married to Tim, and he was having such a negative influence on her life. She met a pastor who was a prior heroin user. She saw drug users and prostitutes on the streets who were crying and giving their lives to Jesus. She had truly seen mankind at its worst, but now she was starting to get exposed to some of the good, as well. When she went to church, they had a Bible verse that spoke to her. It was from the book of Jeremiah, Chapter 29, and verse 11. This encouraging verse filled with hope remains one of her favorite verses to this day. *"For I know the plans I have for you," declares the LORD, "plans to prosper you and not to harm you, plans to give you hope and a future."*

Even though Gale had accepted the Lord at the crusade, she still had questions. "God, are you real?" was a question that Gale asked frequently. Gale was being exposed to God over and over. What Gale didn't understand at the time is that faith isn't something we accept. Rather, faith is something we receive. We don't choose Christ. He chooses us. Christ had already chosen Gale. It was God's nudge, his wake-up call. He had touched her heart with the gospel. The gospel is the good news of Jesus Christ. Because of that, Gale was receiving faith. What an amazing gift God gives us through this means.

At this time in her life, she sought counsel from her Uncle Anthony, who was visiting. He was a minister. "You are God's temple. Are you taking care of God's temple?" he asked. He discussed the physical abuse she was suffering at the hands of Tim. "How can I know God when I am being beaten all the time?" she said. Her Uncle Anthony told her she could stay with him until she could get on her feet. Slowly, she got bank cards and put the title of the car in Tim's name. She started planning an escape to go to her Uncle Anthony's. Slowly, she started saving up some money. It was a scary time. She had one important thing in her favor. God was taking care of her. Gale knew that.

Tim took the house phone out. He kept beating her until Christmas Day in 1985. She had been preparing to leave for a while. A few months earlier, she had already packed some bags and hidden them. She took her packed bags and left Tim on Christmas Day to go be with her sister and family. Gale's parents had given her an old car to drive. She snuck out of the house. The car was parked on a slope, so she wouldn't have to start it right away. She hadn't been with family for the holidays for years.

A few days after Gale left Tim, as she left work, she discovered he had stolen her car. Gale immediately contacted the police. They told her there was a 50-50 chance of her getting her car back. "We can't do anything," they told her. She stayed with her sister, Marsha. During this time, Gale prayed for Tim to be saved. He was furious that she would no longer drink and do drugs with him. He came to see her. He promised her that he would go to work and stop doing drugs. She went back to him. It only lasted a week. He was a controller. He would get jealous if anyone looked at her. She wasn't allowed to go to any family gatherings or even shop alone. She wasn't even allowed to go to her sister's wedding dance.

Making these major life changes was both frightening and exhausting. She didn't want to go back to drinking and doing drugs again. She cried out to God, "How do I do this? Direct my path." Gale cried until she fell asleep.

Soon after that, the time had come. Gale and her Dad had gone out for a Chinese dinner. She apologized to her Dad. She felt she owed him an apology. After all, her mom had told Gale that Gale was the reason the family was so messed up. Her Dad apologized to Gale for not being there for her.

One day, Gale came home from work. Tim came in. He was stoned, as usual. It confirmed for her that it was okay to be leaving for a second time. She had her suitcases hidden at a friend's. The time had come to make a clean break of it. After eight years of marriage, she left Tim. She left everything she had behind except for a few clothes in some suitcases. She left with nothing except her faith and a nudge from God. A nudge that was leading her to make God the center of her life. A nudge that was going to make her physically healthier and mentally stronger. A nudge that was going to completely change the direction of her life and her motivation. A nudge that would allow her to truly belong to God and serve him by making him first in her life.

Gale took the train from California to Oregon to stay at her Uncle Anthony's house. Gale was met by her uncle at the station. Life was beginning to look brighter.

Gale longed to go back to Big Grandma and Little Grandma's in Wisconsin. After all, her stay at her uncle's place was only temporary. After some time at her Uncle Anthony's, Gale got a call that Great-Grandma was in the hospital dying. Gale decided she wanted to buy a plane ticket to Wisconsin. As she priced out the ticket, she was amazed. The ticket cost $386.00. That is exactly what was in her checkbook! Nudged! Gale was trusting in God and starting to recognize his hand in her life. She longed to follow him and live her life as he wanted her to. She quit her job and bought a plane ticket to Wisconsin.

Once back in Wisconsin, Gale had much more family around her. Gale went to visit Grandma Engel. As Gale walked into the hospital room, she recognized that her Grandma Engel's life would soon be over. Grandma Engel was saying the Lord's Prayer over and over again in German. "She's not scared," Gale thought. "She knows where she's going." Something was happening deep within Gale's soul. Yes, Gale was being nudged yet again!

Gale stayed in Wisconsin for Grandma Engel's funeral. After the funeral, Gale re-connected with Ryan and found out that he was divorced also.

Thankfully, Gale had some healing occurring. There was still the unfinished matter of all the hurt and abandonment by her mother. Eventually, Gale found happiness with Ryan, her first love. They got married and moved out of state. The babies started coming. Gale was blessed with five children.

Gale soon learned that being a mom is one of the greatest blessings a woman can have. It can also be one of the greatest worries and challenges a woman can have. We want to protect our children from the bad things of this world. We want to shield them from being hurt. We rock them and comfort them when they are little. We worry about their safety. We walk the floor at night when they have a fever. We put bandages on when they get hurt. We help with homework that is not at all like our homework was. We ache when they are bullied at school. We hope they choose the right friends. We pray for them to be saved. We want them to turn away from the temptations of the world. And yet, God would not have us worry. He is in control. He knows what parenting is all about. After all, our Heavenly Father has the biggest family of all to look after.

Gale turned to the Lord to help lighten her burden of worry. She remembered how she had been the victim of bullying when she was growing up. She thought about the terrible experiences during her school years. She remembered how some of the schools had failed her. She remembered how her mom had failed her. Gale couldn't bear the thought of any of her children going through what she had. She knew she couldn't do all she wanted to do to keep her children safe. She knew that there was only one who could. As she grew in her faith, she realized the power of prayer. What a blessing to be able to turn everything over to God!

As Gale practiced the power of prayer, she kept a journal. Marsha told Gale about a prayer group and sent her information about it. The prayer group was called Moms in Touch. It was later renamed to Moms in Prayer International. This was when she really launched the power of prayer in her life. Previously, she didn't really understand that prayer was speaking to God from the heart. She thought of prayer as reciting table blessings or bedtime prayers. She didn't understand that you could actually talk to God.

There had been some problems in the school Gale's children attended. She was concerned about the direction things were going. Remembering all that she had gone through growing up, she felt this was of great importance.

She got the information to start a Mom's in Prayer group in her area. They met every Friday. They gave praise, thanks, confessed their sins, and prayed for protection for their children in school and for the school their children attended. They prayed for their children to be saved and safe. The group started with four moms praying weekly. Two other moms called each other and prayed on the phone together. The group prayed for fifteen years. Now, there's a group of praying grandmothers.

They prayed for the children of the school district. This opened the door to communication and awareness of the need for prayer. Some people would approach her and tell her that specific prayers were needed. Everything was handled with strict confidence. With the prayers, they saw positive results. Gale watched the women she prayed with and saw their struggles. She learned more about how to pray. These women came together and formed a friendship. Gale noticed God doing powerful things in their lives and hers. If she wouldn't have become a member of this group, she wouldn't have learned from these women. She wouldn't have learned about growing her faith and using the power of prayer and God's Word in your life. She wouldn't have learned about a daily walk with God.

What a blessing the prayer group was to so many families, so many students, and the school system itself. God was at work. He truly was in control. The praying moms had given their children one of the best gifts possible. They turned their children over to the Lord. No matter what came their way, their children were protected by an invisible bubble. Their Heavenly Father had his eye on them, even when mom was out of sight.

Again, truly I tell you that
if two of you on earth agree about anything they ask for,
it will be done for them by my Father in heaven.
For where two or three gather in my name,
there am I with them."

Matthew 18:19-20 NIV

Gale feels that without the power of this praying group of moms, her children would have had a much higher chance of engaging in doing drugs and drinking alcohol. They didn't. Instead, they chose their friends carefully and took care of their friends, sometimes even bringing them home. (To learn more about Moms in Prayer International, you can visit their website at www.MomsInPrayer.org.)

Many years later, aging took its toll and Gale's Dad was ill. The doctors said he couldn't travel anymore. Soon, they would be doing a long-distance move, bringing Gale's mom and dad back home and helping to care for them. Gale and her sister tried to talk to their mother. They didn't get anywhere with that conversation. It all seemed so hopeless to get any kind of closure to their pain. They tried to tell her how she had hurt them. Again, their mother failed to acknowledge her shortcomings. Again, they were left with their unresolved wounds. The only healing was recognizing that their mom had an illness.

By now, Gale was desperate for some kind of healing and resolution. She started reading…a lot. She was always searching for self-help books and praying for a close relationship.

Now, she was beginning to understand why her mother never "got" it. Why did her mother never hurt for her or feel the need to rescue and comfort her and be supportive during all of her childhood traumas? She realized her mom was narcissistic. In the eyes of a narcissistic mother, nothing or no one is more important than them. They can't relate to what is happening to their children because their entire focus is on themselves.

God was working on Gale's heart. With her new understanding clearing up some of the confusion about the relationship with her mother, she changed her focus. Gale stopped looking at herself, her shortcomings, and her life challenges. Gale received healing from Jesus and decided to help others. She knew as a child of God it was time to start thinking in terms of what she could do for others.

She learned many things. She learned that if you rely only on people, they won't fill you up, may hurt you, and cause you pain. You don't have to let people hurt you. It's okay. God is the one to rely on. He will fill you up. Gale learned that seeking God is huge.

Besides reading the Bible, Gale read many faith-based books to help her in her journey. She did this to teach her and guide her because her upbringing gave her nothing to draw on. She learned about the foundations of a healthy family and raising kids in love while encouraging and guiding them. She knew from her own experiences that God can help us do anything, even if we come from a messed up family.

She had to go through a lot to get the door open. She always wanted to control everything until she gave herself to Christ. It was then that she said, "Okay, God, take over!" A big life lesson for Gale was that just because you are a Christian, that doesn't mean that life is going to be easy. This led Gale to recognize that yes, people are watching us. People do notice how we live our lives and how we respond to things. She also recognizes that we have all fallen. We need to stay focused. The words of Isaiah 40:29-31 resonated with her and quickly became her favorite scripture.

He gives strength to the weary
and increases the power of the weak.
Even youths grow tired and weary,
and young men stumble and fall;
but those who hope in the LORD
will renew their strength.
They will soar on wings like eagles;
they will run and not grow weary,
they will walk and not be faint.

Isaiah 40:29-31 NIV

Gale learned at an early age that life was tough. It was cruel. God took a little girl who was sexually abused, a child who was abandoned and neglected by her mother, a teen who was bullied, an adult who was seeking and doing drugs and physically abused, and all the while searching...for what, she did not know. He took her on a journey through perilous times and gave her Jesus. He used all the pain, neglect, abuse, and horror she had experienced for the greater good. He was preparing the soil of her heart and enriching it with the fertilizer of his Word so that his Holy Spirit could take root. He let her experience the pain of all those things, and then he revealed his love and comfort to her. But why? Could it be he was preparing her for a greater mission? Could it be he had plans to use her to support others on their earthly journey? When his time was right, he planted the seed. Nourished by his word and his love, she blossomed.

With all that she had endured, she could relate to the hard times other people sometimes have to go through in this world. She had first-hand knowledge from which she could speak. She also had God in her heart. She was an overcomer. God nudged her. God had given her some missions. And she accepted those missions. She helped lead others to Christ. She encouraged fellow believers. She harnessed the power of prayer, which helped change many children's lives. And somehow, we don't think God is done giving her missions. He's put a lot of work into his special creation. He knows this servant will continue to accept his missions.

Gale has been on a lifelong journey. It has taken her through rugged territory and caused her to fight the enemy. The road hasn't been easy. While on that journey, she has had many nudges. Through God's nudges, she conquered drugs and alcohol, escaped abuse, raised a family, and spiritually supported others. Most importantly, she has learned what matters most in life.

Gale's long journey took her on unfamiliar paths. When times were dark, God shone his light. When the road was rough, he made it smooth. When others forsook her, he did not. After that journey, that long, hard journey, she found what her heart had longed for all that time. She treasured what she had found. She didn't want to waste the heartaches and lessons she had learned on her journey.

God took a broken, abandoned girl and during that journey, he transformed her into a strong Christian woman. God had given her a treasure to share with others from that journey. Her long journey to Jesus.

⁓

I will lead the blind by ways they have not known,
along unfamiliar paths I will guide them;
I will turn the darkness into light before them
and make the rough places smooth.
These are the things I will do;
I will not forsake them.

Isaiah 42:16 NIV

⁓

Pause to Ponder

Gale's life was spiraling out of control from childhood on. She didn't know what normal was. She was living in a dysfunctional family. Although she went to church and knew of her Savior, she didn't really know him. Although she didn't know what at first, she knew she was searching for something. She was searching for a real relationship with Jesus, which was very difficult to find amongst all the turmoil in her young life.

She felt alone, even in a crowd, until she was exposed to seeing how people in a real relationship with God lived. She quietly watched and learned from them: a persistent friend and co-worker, two loving grandmothers, her surrogate mothers, and the group of praying moms. Despite the horrific childhood events she endured, God always sent someone to be around, to be an example, to teach her of his ways, to protect her. And, in God's time, he wrapped his loving arms around this broken woman and brought her back to him. He nudged her many times.

Not only did he save her, but he used all the hurt, all the brokenness and pain to equip her for the life she lives today. He made her a strong Christian woman. He's given her many callings to help others. She recognizes that and focuses on serving others and sharing the faith that she once was searching for.

Gale also had a calling to be an advocate for her children and others when they were in school. Gale went from being the kid in the awful school, the kid who was bullied, the kid who was let down time and again by school officials and by her mom, to being an advocate for her own kids and other kids through Moms in Prayer. God took Gale full circle from being the one in need of help to being the one seeking to help others. She used what she had learned to try to spare others from going through the pain she had endured in her early years. She also used what she had learned about the importance of a meaningful and deep faith to help the most vulnerable...our children. God used many people in her life to help make this happen.

Ponder on this: Who were the anchor people in your Christian faith? Who influenced you when you needed faith? Would you be where you are today in your faith life if these anchor people hadn't been there for you?

Whose life could God use you to help? Who might end up a lost soul if you don't step up and fulfill the mission God has for you? We've all got at least one in our life, right? That lost and searching soul. Now that you have thought about this, what would your first step be to share the love and hope in Christ that person so desperately needs? Go ahead, be their anchor, then throw them the lifesaver ring found in the gospel. Pray that the Holy Spirit would nudge their heart. Is there anything that you feel a need to do? Is God nudging you? Yes, I thought so!

Pause for Prayer

Dear Lord,

Sometimes we carry wounds from our childhood. Those wounds can cause separation from you. Please heal us of those wounds. Remove any bitterness we may harbor. Cause our faith to be strengthened, to grow, to gain depth.

Help us to help others to grow in their faith, and where there is no faith, help us to lead them to you. Help us to share with others how a life with you offers solutions to all of their problems and peace and contentment for their soul. Remind us how much you care for us. Forgive us for sins that would lead us on another path away from you.

Our children and grandchildren are so precious to us and to you. We cannot always be there to protect them. Just as you gave us these precious ones to love and care for, may we entrust them back in your care knowing that we can only do so much as earthly parents. Help us remember to use the power of prayer in our life, especially for our children and grandchildren. Please help them to come to know and accept you as their Savior.

When children have been neglected, mistreated, or abused, we know that the effect can be life-long. Please bring these children peace and comfort. Help heal them with your love and forgiveness. Help them to forgive those who have wronged them. Replace their pain with a burning desire to serve you and others. Fill their hearts with your love.

In Jesus's name.
Amen.

CHAPTER 14

Content With Life's Blessings

Life was good. "I enjoy life," Adaline often repeats that sentiment as she reminisces about her family and her life. It was a family blessed. Over eighty years ago, she was born in the Midwest. Her grandfather had been a Lutheran minister. Her father had been a teacher, principal, and football coach, earning $2,000 annually. During the summer, he worked on his father-in-law's farm. That is where he met his future wife. Adaline's parents were later married and started a family. Adaline remembers her father discussing his career. After so many years of teaching and trying to raise a family on those wages, he said there wasn't enough money in teaching. He bought the local Coast to Coast store. Being very involved in church, he experienced the excitement of helping to build a new church. Although her father was not very demonstrative, her mother was very loving.

Adaline grew up and married George, a very patient and loving man. He was brought up in the Lutheran faith. His dad was a parochial school teacher. Her father-in-law played the organ for over forty years. Being a gifted musician, he wrote a song for George and Adaline's wedding. What a special gift that was!

As happens to many people as they enter the later years of their life, Adaline finds her circle of family and friends has grown smaller. Her husband has been gone for many years. His three brothers and his sister are all gone. These losses leave a noticeable void in life.

Despite Adaline's blessed life, she still faced some challenges, as we all do. Life is never perfect while living on this earth. Adaline had one daughter and two sons. Adaline reminisces about life when her children were small. She was a busy young mother raising her family. Her daughter, Nicole, had Scarlet Fever when she was in Kindergarten. She was a small child. Several years later when Nicole was in fourth grade, she was enjoying playtime with the neighbor girl. The neighbor girl's dad watched the girls playing. He happened to be a doctor from Holland. The doctor had some concerns. He told Adaline that something major was wrong with her daughter. He wasn't sure what it was, but she needed to get it checked out right away. It turned out that Adaline's daughter had a playdate diagnosis, thanks to her observant neighbor.

Adaline's daughter was sent to Madison, Wisconsin, for a medical evaluation. The doctors determined that she had been born with a heart defect. The doctors told her that Nicole's aorta was the size of a pin where it should have been the size of her little finger. She was small for her age, and they couldn't do the surgery until she got bigger. It was serious. It was a long wait, but finally, between eighth grade and her freshman year of high school, Nicole had surgery. They sewed her aorta together with her heart. She was in the hospital for a month. When she was 50, her aorta ballooned where they had attached it to her heart. She had to have another surgery...this time in Kansas City. That aorta wore out, and they had to do yet another surgery when she was 64. This time, she went to a major heart institute. After her surgery, they couldn't get her heart started. They ended up putting in a pacemaker. Nicole was a strong Christian woman and relied on the Lord to get her through these trying times.

Adaline and her family had always been strong in faith, but these health challenges of her daughter's increased their faith and prayer life. It brought the family even closer together.

Now, after seven years of independent living, Adaline enjoys being as active as she can be. She looks forward to her annual get-together with her surviving cousins. Family is important to her. Despite the challenges of macular degeneration, she doesn't complain. She makes adjustments using large-print reading materials and books on audio. She pushes forward, going shopping with her sister. She attends church and multiple Bible studies. She goes walking, as the vision changes make driving more and more challenging.

Adaline's positive attitude is an important component of her life. When she starts feeling down, she prays. Soon after she prays, she feels more upbeat.

Adaline has an attitude of gratitude for the many positive things in her life. Faith is a very big part of her life. She is thankful that her brother and sister both married Christians.

Some of us have to get to a certain stage of life to appreciate all that we have and all that we have experienced. But then there are others who recognize and appreciate their blessings all through their life. Adaline recognizes the blessings God has showered on her. While some families struggle with a mix of different faiths in the same household or no faith at all in some family members, she has been blessed with a united family. They are united in faith. They all are Christians. They all are Lutheran. They are all members of the same church body with the same beliefs. They are spared the faith-based conflicts found in some families. Adaline has lived a blessed life. She acknowledges she has received these blessings from God. She recognizes it. She appreciates it. She shares her thankfulness with anyone who will listen.

As the years have advanced, Adaline finds herself in the golden years. You certainly wouldn't think that watching and listening to her. Adaline seems quite young at heart.

"I am ready to go, anytime," she will frequently say. And she doesn't say that in a sad way. That's not something we are used to hearing people say. She has no qualms about leaving all her earthly blessings behind. For all the blessings of this world that Adaline has enjoyed, she knows the best is waiting for her in heaven. She looks forward to the day when she will share the joys of being with her Savior in heaven. She looks forward to that reunion that is to come with her loved ones. Meanwhile, she lives in contentment. She practices a thankful heart and thanks God for all his blessings, for she knows all those blessings came from him. It is good to have a young, thankful, joyful heart.

❧

The Lord has done great things for us,
and we are filled with joy.

Psalm 126:3 NIV

❧

Pause to Ponder

Need a nudge? Adaline is joyful in the Lord. She oozes thankfulness and gratitude for all the blessings he has provided. She does this regularly and every chance she gets in talking with others. She lives in contentment. How many people do you know who live in contentment? Is that an easy thing to do while living on this earth? How often do you express to others your appreciation for all God has done for you and given you? How often do you tell God of your gratitude? Are you feeling a little nudge to start letting your thankfulness be heard by God and others? How can you do that? If you don't know how, ask him!

Pause for Prayer

Dear Lord,

All too often, we turn our prayers into a list of our wants and needs. Please help us to remember to also use our prayers as a way to thank and praise you. Thank you for all of the good things you bring to us in life. Thank you for the happy times and special things you provide for us. Thank you for providing for our daily needs. Thank you for our health. Instead of always seeking more, help us to be content with what we have. Help us to truly appreciate what you have given us and not take it for granted. Give us joyful, thankful, and contented hearts.

In Jesus's name.
Amen.

CHAPTER 15

The Fear Is Gone

She had been a Christian all her life. Even so, she didn't feel like she was acting like a Christian at that point in her life. She wasn't actively reading the Bible. She didn't feel like she was being led by the Holy Spirit. Elena was going through the motions of life. Yes, that was it. She felt like she was living on auto-pilot.

Like many others, she wondered about death. She thought about it at times. And yes, she was afraid of dying. She had been ever since she was a little girl. Elena wasn't obsessed with this fear of death. It wasn't a debilitating fear, but she wasn't comfortable with the thought of dying either. Just the same, Elena believed heaven was real.

It was 1992. It was a busy time in her life. Elena had a career as an Emergency Medical Technician. Yes, she had seen some things. She had a two-year-old son at home. Now she was in the hospital with her newborn twin boys.

It was the morning after the twins were born when it happened. Elena's uterus ruptured. She heard them read her vitals. She knew she was in trouble. The numbers were bottoming out. She was bleeding out. She had no doubt about it. Her EMT experience told her that they were losing her with those numbers.

She heard the staff calling the clergy for her. "I'm Lutheran," Elena said. "Get me a Lutheran pastor."

They were going to have to do an emergency hysterectomy to try to save her. As the medical personnel moved into crisis mode, they started speeding her cart down the hall toward the operating room.

"Jesus, I need your help," Elena cried out. "You're my Savior. I need your help!"

Immediately, she was surrounded by a warm white light. She felt a wonderful sense of peace. There was no fear. Elena knew that she was going home. And home wasn't a physical address on this earth. Home was heaven! She didn't recognize it as heaven at that moment. But she knew she was going home.

Although she didn't necessarily recognize who they were, Elena knew that she was around people who loved her. It was a beautiful, indescribable feeling. Along with the wonderful love she felt, the feeling of peace was something she will never forget. She loved experiencing that peace. It was what she had read of in the Bible. The peace that surpasses all understanding. This was certainly a place she wanted to be.

But then Elena heard the words she wasn't sure she wanted to hear. "You can't go yet. Those twins need you," said the voice. Immediately, she was whooshed back into this world. These things all happened in a moment, or at least what seemed like a moment.

The doctors performed the emergency surgery and got the bleeding stopped. Physically, Elena was going to be alright. As she lay in the recovery room, she slowly started waking up. She found herself very disappointed to be waking up in this world after experiencing the love and peace she had felt earlier. She really wanted to go back to that place of peace.

As she lay there in her post-surgery grogginess, Elena heard staff talking about a woman who had lost her uterus. She felt sorry for the woman who would no longer be able to have children. She empathized with that woman as she, also, wanted to have a girl someday to add to her family. Later, Elena learned the woman they were talking about was her. She was sad that the little girl she longed for wasn't to be. She thought about the voice telling her that she couldn't go yet…the twins needed her.

Elena did not fear death when this was happening, and she doesn't fear death now. She knows that God has more work for her here. She thinks of this whenever she feels disappointed about having to come back to this earth. Her near-death experience helps her not to worry about those who have passed before her in Christ. Although she may miss them, she knows she need not worry about them.

In the days, weeks, and months that followed, it was easy to give in to the feelings that she wasn't making a difference. Sometimes, we feel like we aren't making the mark. But then Elena remembered what had happened. She had felt the fullness of God in that moment.

At the time, this experience didn't change anything other than Elena lost her fear of dying. She felt the comfort of the 23rd Psalm.

Even though I walk through the darkest valley,
I will fear no evil, for you are with me;
Your rod and your staff, they comfort me.

Psalm 23:4 NIV

She still went to church, but she hadn't started reading the Bible yet at that point. There were good things and sad things happening in her life at that time. She was very busy raising her twins and a two-year-old. She had an imminent divorce and a busy career. Like many other young people, she was busy with life.

Even so, God was at work on her. He reminded her that he was in charge. He reminded her that it isn't necessary to fear death. He was laying the groundwork for a life of faith and trust in him. He was also laying the groundwork for her to witness to others for him. Yes, God was in control. He wanted Elena to be here for some important work he had set aside for her.

Elena has no doubt. She trusts that when her loved ones die in faith, they are with the Lord. She is comforted knowing that they are in heaven. She often witnesses to others that she called on the name of the Lord. She tells others that she experienced the peace that surpasses all understanding and that heaven is real. She comforts those who face the grieving process with their loved ones.

This faithful servant does this work for the Lord as she patiently waits for the day she can return to that place of peace. She knows that when her work here is done and when that day comes, God will let her stay. He will let her stay at home. Her real home in heaven.

God nudged Elena with a precious reminder. She knows that when she dies, she will live! She will live forever in that indescribable place of peace and love.

And the peace of God, which transcends all understanding,
will guard your hearts and your minds in Christ Jesus.

Philippians 4:7 NIV

Pause to Ponder

Have you ever been to a fancy ice cream shop? Have you ever been given a pink spoon? The pink spoon is a small spoon that is used to provide a free taste of a particular flavor of ice cream. If the customer likes it, they want more. They want the full serving. Imagine if after having a taste of that excellent ice cream, the shopkeeper told you they were all out of that flavor and that you'll have to come back another day. That leaves you disappointed, waiting, and wanting more for quite some time.

God had given Elena a pink spoon. He gave her a taste, a sample. She liked that taste. She wanted more. But God has control of the ice cream scoop. Elena understood that if she believed and followed him, when he determined it was her time to go home to heaven, he would give her a full serving. Until then, Elena must remember that wonderful pink spoon sample she had. It was so good. She knew that God had more work for her to do. He wanted her to raise her sons. He wanted her to tell others about her pink spoon experience. She looks forward to a full serving when God says it is time.

Despite the trials and disappointments in this life, we know that something far better awaits believers. God's Word promises that. God's Pink Spooners agree.

Pause for Prayer

Dear Lord,

We've all had those times. We've all had times when we see someone suffering and dying and we wonder about what is to come. We wonder, when it is time for us to leave this world, will we linger and suffer? We wonder, will there be pain? We wonder if we will pass away in our sleep. We wonder if we will be alert and able to communicate with our loved ones. When we are anxious, calm us. Give us your reassurance through your Word.

We sometimes forget to focus on what you have promised to believers. We have much to look forward to!

As we think about what is to come, help us to focus on what you would have us do for you here and now. Keep us mindful of the tasks you set before us. Remind us of your promise that you will be with us always. Remind us of your protection and comfort, even when we walk through the valley of the shadow of death. When it is our time, take us home to be with you in heaven forever.

Your Word gives us much assurance of the important things concerning what is to come. Sometimes, we even wonder if we have been good enough to make it to heaven, our real home. Yes, sometimes we forget what really allows us entry to heaven. Remind us that you sent your Son, Jesus, to save us from our sins so that we can live with you forever in heaven. Give us peace as we ponder these things. Help us to be reading the Bible and wrapping ourselves in the comfort of your promises.

In Jesus's name.
Amen.

CHAPTER 16

A Walk in Forgiveness

Living in a small town in Indiana, Abigail was involved in many community and church activities. She was happy, outgoing, and a fun personality to be around.

After a long illness, Abigail's husband of over fifty years passed away from cancer. While grieving the loss of her husband, Abigail knew the pain of loneliness. She missed the companionship of her husband. In time, she found companionship again and got married. She felt blessed to have Paul in her life.

Sometimes, things happen that we can't understand. The answers just aren't always available. Abigail quickly learned that as much as we think we know someone before we marry them, sometimes we don't really know them until we have been together as man and wife for a period of time.

Although Paul went to church with Abigail, over time things came up in conversations that made her concerned about his faith and beliefs. He eventually told her that he did not believe in God.

This was not an easy thing to deal with. But perhaps God had a plan to use Abigail.

Early on in the marriage, Paul became verbally abusive to Abigail. She was constantly watched and continuously receiving critiques about everything she did. Big things. Little everyday things. It was non-stop criticism. Abigail's self-esteem plummeted. She could no longer be herself.

She wanted to do what was right in God's eyes, yet with the serious toll this situation was taking on her; she wasn't sure she was going to be able to stay in the marriage. Abigail talked to her family about the situation. Her life was changing, and it wasn't for the better. She talked to her pastor about it, also. The pastor had to counsel by the Bible. And the Bible clearly states divorce is not what we are to be doing. This conflict caused much inner turmoil for Abigail.

Day after day, the mental abuse continued. Day after day, Abigail's smile and sparkle faded. Abigail was losing herself. She was torn about what to do. Her husband became more and more possessive of her. He was very judgmental. He believed everyone was wrong but him. He only knew his work, and he worked by himself. He placed the blame on others for everything.

Abigail often thought about her situation. The mental abuse was taking a toll on her health. She again consulted with the pastor. He understood the toll this was taking on her, yet he had to counsel based on the biblical perspective. Abigail continued to struggle with the situation. She felt that from a biblical perspective, she should stay married to him, even though it was a mentally abusive relationship.

For so many couples in crisis, there is fear. Fear of what is happening to them. Fear of making the right choice. There was also a heavy sense of responsibility for obeying God and doing what is right. And there was another issue. When marriages are on the brink, couples are concerned about what others will think. Will they be judged? Physical abuse shows on the outside to others. It is easier for people to understand and deal with. Mental and emotional abuse are mostly unseen by others. It becomes a "He-Said, She Said" situation. That was hard to deal with, too.

Abigail eventually got Paul to go with her to get marriage counseling, but he did not listen to the counselors. Things were only getting worse for her. In time, Abigail's children stopped coming home because of Paul.

After ten years of marriage, it was getting to be too difficult. Abigail was now more isolated than ever. Abigail talked to those closest to her about the situation. Abigail's mind played her mother's voice in her head. She had always said, "You made your bed, now lie in it." Meanwhile, her sister told her that her mother would want her to be happy. Her niece told her she can't live in that situation. People weighed in with their opinions. Some chose sides. Some judged. Still, the desire to obey God's will was in the foreground. Abigail knew that 1 Corinthians 13:5 gave her some guidance regarding love. It does not dishonor others; it is not self-seeking; it is not easily angered, and it keeps no record of wrongs. The struggle to obey God was real. So was the struggle to protect herself.

Abigail was feeling mentally beaten down. She tried talking to Paul, hoping to change the situation. But nothing changed. She and Paul separated. One Sunday, Paul came to Sunday services. As Paul left church, Abigail followed him to try to talk to him. As the pastor saw this, he smiled at Abigail and nodded, hoping that Abigail would succeed in changing the situation. Unfortunately, nothing changed. Eventually, she decided to get a divorce simply as a matter of self-preservation.

Abigail has accepted God's plan and trusts in him to take care of the situation. She isn't sure what God's plan is. Often, believers find that to be the case. After the divorce, she discovered that Paul was continuing to go to church and sitting in the back. He did so despite the fact that he had confessed to Abigail that he was an atheist. Abigail was fascinated by that, as he was driving quite a distance to attend those services. She gave thanks for that. She prayed that the

Holy Spirit would someday change his heart and lead Paul to become a believer.

Despite the difficulties of divorce, a blessing came out of it. God was at work. He nudged Abigail to forgive Paul. She is grateful she was able to find it in her heart to forgive him. She knows she could not have done that on her own but only through the work of the Holy Spirit. Sometimes, when we have been wronged, we have to work toward forgiveness. It takes real effort. Trying over and over. Saying the words over and over until we believe them and buy into it. Making it take within our hearts. It's similar to creating a new healthy habit. It takes repetition. Where bitterness could easily take root, God's love and the Holy Spirit can cause our hearts to make that effort to forgive.

Forgiveness is one of the more difficult things to do in life. As forgiveness is given, it is given not just once, not just seven times, but seventy-seven times or however many times we need to, until it takes. Forgiveness mends two hearts…the one belonging to the person we forgive and our own heart.

Then Peter came to Jesus and asked,
"Lord, how many times shall I forgive
my brother or sister who sins against me?
Up to seven times?"
Jesus answered,
"I tell you, not seven times, but seventy-seven times."

Matthew 18:21-22 NIV

Pause to Ponder

As we face trials on this earth, we struggle with making decisions and moving on with our life. We sometimes wonder why these hurtful things happen to us. We need time and opportunities to heal. Our heart may be broken. Our spirit may be suffering.

It is then that the Great Physician has the opportunity to perform open heart surgery on us if we let him. He can fix our broken hearts if we ask him. As he closes the incision, he opens up his heavenly medicine chest and covers the wound with the soothing antiseptic of forgiveness if we ask him to.

God's open heart surgery benefits us and the person we need to forgive. God's physician services are freely given to us in love. No worries about insurance. No co-pays.

Is there anyone you need to forgive? God is now taking appointments for open-heart surgery.

Pause for Prayer

Dear Lord,

We do our best for you. Yet sometimes we feel like our best isn't enough. Sometimes, the circumstances we find ourselves in don't lend themselves to a clear or easy path to follow you and serve you. We may feel conflicted. Help us to navigate those difficult paths with clear and obvious answers. Strengthen us when we grow weary. When someone treats us badly, give us forgiving hearts despite the pain we are feeling. Help us to navigate these difficult situations in a way that we can honor and please you in our response.

We ask these things in Jesus's name.
Amen.

CHAPTER 17

Miraculous Healing

It was time for Grace's annual physical. At ninety-plus years old, she thought she was in fairly good condition, with the exception of some toe amputations, which required her to use a walker. The usual physical was completed with a round of blood tests.

A few days later, the phone rang. It was the doctor's office. Grace needed to come back for a follow-up visit. At the follow-up visit, she received some concerning news. Her white blood cell count was off—way off. The doctors were concerned. It didn't sound good.

Grace was sent to oncology. They performed a bone marrow test. The doctor said that Grace had a type of blood cancer. The doctor continued to monitor Grace's blood tests. For six tests, the white cell count continued to be way off. Imagine the thoughts going through most people's minds after having that many serious test results. Imagine the dread of the lab work and the doctor visits and what one might be told. Imagine waiting to hear about the prognosis and the upcoming medical plan to treat the cancer.

Grace was not rattled. Throughout this process, she turned her concerns over to the Lord. She prayed a simple and powerful prayer for healing. "Dear Jesus," she said, "I know that you healed people when you walked on this earth, and I know you can heal me now." Grace had faith and trusted that God would take care of her. Despite having six tests with very concerning results, Grace still had faith.

Soon it was time to check the lab work again. The seventh round of tests brought unexpected results—at least to the doctors. There was no evidence of the cancer in her blood tests! Imagine the doctor's surprise. How could this be? This was a shock to the medical community. They weren't used to seeing something like this.

From the very beginning of her medical dilemma, Grace had her priorities right. Grace understood an important teaching. Never underestimate the power of God. He is omnipotent. He is capable of doing things far greater than we can even imagine. No disease is too much for him to overcome if that is his will. Could that be why he is sometimes referred to as the Great Physician?

Yes, the doctors were quite surprised at Grace's healing. But with the faith that she had, perhaps it wasn't such a surprise to Grace. Grace knows that faith in God is good medicine for her soul.

❧

Then he said to her,
"Daughter, your faith has healed you. Go in peace."

Luke 8:48 NIV

❧

If you believe, you will receive whatever you ask for in prayer.

Matthew 21:22 NIV

Pause to Ponder

Having a serious illness can be devastating. There are many things that go through our minds as we face the possibilities. How long do we have? Will we have to go through treatments? Will there be side effects? Should we get our affairs in order? Will we be a burden to the family? How outrageous will the medical bills be? Will we endure pain and suffering? One never knows how one will respond until facing a serious illness. Prayer and trust in God is of primary importance. Now is the time to lean on the best support available to mankind. Now is the time to let him catch us when we grow faint or weary. Trust.

Pause for Prayer

Dear Lord,

Sometimes we are faced with health challenges. Some of these challenges make getting around and doing our normal day-to-day functions difficult or impossible. Sometimes, we have ailments that cause us distress and pain. Some are afflicted with a silent disease that often goes undetected until it is life-threatening. When we have ailments, help us to put our faith and trust in you. Heal us from our infirmities, Lord. Grant us peace in those trying moments. Increase our faith. Help us to keep our trust and focus on you always. Help us to pray expectantly. Help us tell others what you have done for us.

In Jesus's name.
Amen.

CHAPTER 18

Addiction Intervention

It was the cool thing to do. That was why she started. She discovered she really enjoyed it. Mel had been a smoker since she was 23 years old. She knew she should quit. She wanted to quit. But, she just couldn't quit. Dealing with addictions can be a real challenge.

Mel found that smoking was comforting to her. Did I tell you... she really enjoyed it? It soon became a habit. She would have a cigarette in the morning with her coffee. She would have a cigarette when it was break time at work. She would even have a cigarette when she was paying the bills. There were many other times and circumstances that just fit with smoking. It even helped when Mel would feel stressed. She mostly smoked for the comfort she found in it.

Mel tried to quit smoking once after her daughter was born. As often happens with nicotine addictions, she was unable to stay away from the cigarettes for very long and soon resumed smoking. That's how it was for 45 years. A cigarette with the morning coffee to get the day started, and throughout each day and night.

Mel was about one year away from retirement. She had been praying and praying for God to help her quit. The challenge of giving up a lifelong habit of smoking proved to be over-powering. Still, she continued to ask God to help her to quit.

Suddenly, Mel became very ill. She had become very dehydrated. She also had a severe Urinary Tract Infection. It was so bad she was admitted to the hospital. Mel felt awful. The nurse came to put in a needle for an IV. Over and over, she tried to insert the needle into the vein. Over and over, she missed the vein. This is a painful ordeal in itself, on top of being so ill. Mel's husband couldn't bear to watch the repeated attempts to get the needle into the vein when his wife was already suffering so much. He told them if they didn't get the vein on the next try, they needed to get someone else to do the job. The nurse tried again, this time with success. Mel was so sick she didn't even care about the repeated attempts at inserting the needle. She was so sick; she didn't even care about the pain.

While at the hospital, Mel could have gone out for smoke breaks, but somehow, she just didn't feel up to it. She started wondering if maybe this was God's way of helping her to give up smoking.

While she was in the hospital, she had to have her lungs x-rayed. She was so ill that she didn't even recall why they x-rayed her lungs. The doctors found a shadow on her lungs. Perhaps it was a mass… they really weren't sure. They did a test on her and still could not be sure what they were seeing. The doctors decided to do a biopsy on her lungs. As the doctor inserted the biopsy device in several areas of her lungs, a nurse leaned in near Mel. "They can't find anything, which is good," she quietly said to help reassure Mel. But the doctors appeared to still have concerns. They decided to do another test in a month for further examination. After three days in the hospital, Mel was released to go home.

Meanwhile, God was at work on Mel. God had set the stage to help her quit smoking when she had to be admitted to the hospital for a urinary tract infection. But, just to make sure, and just to ensure this change of habits "stuck", God took it a step further.

After she got home, Mel thought about the situation. "I've gone three days without smoking. I've done this much. I had better not do any more smoking." Mel quit. Totally. Completely. One hundred percent. What they call "Cold Turkey." It takes a long time to not want a cigarette. Once in a while, she would still like a cigarette, but she stuck it out.

The monthlong wait was agony for Mel and her husband. What would the doctors find when they retested her? Meanwhile, Mel was scared. She did not smoke. After one month, the doctors retested Mel. The black shadow on her lungs was gone! The x-ray was clear. Mel hasn't smoked since. She really feels she could not have given up her addiction to smoking if God had not intervened. God took one illness and a potential second serious illness and turned it into an answer to prayer!

❧

I can do all this through him who gives me strength.

Philippians 4:13 NIV

❧

Pause to Ponder

Do you have any bad habits or addictions that are harmful to you or others? Do you treat your body as a temple? Have you taken it to the Lord in prayer? Have you put your trust in him to free you of that harmful habit? Ask him for help. Then do your best and wait patiently, trusting he has a plan for you. When that answer to prayer comes, don't forget to say thanks!

Pause for Prayer

Dear Heavenly Father,

Dealing with addictions can be so difficult. We want to overcome them, but they take such a hold on us. They affect us in so many ways. Please help us to be able to conquer these things that we don't need in our lives. Help us to stop these habits that contribute to health problems. We recognize that by ourselves, we are helpless, but with you, we can overcome them. We thank you, Lord, for the strength you give us to be overcomers.

In Jesus's name.
Amen.

CHAPTER 19

A Friend in Christ

There is nothing quite like a friend. There's a special bond and closeness. You can't wait to see each other. You look forward to phone calls. You plan activities together. And you love to talk to each other and share your deepest concerns. Friends truly are a blessing from God. When you share something in common, the friendship seems intricately woven together, especially when that common thread is a relationship with God.

The spring thaw and sunshine were lifting Katherine's spirits after a snowy Wisconsin winter. She cheerfully scurried to finish a few chores before heading to her sister-in-law's house. They got together every week for coffee and conversation. As she worked on those chores, she found some words repeatedly floating through her mind. "This is the day the Lord has made; let us rejoice and be glad in it." Not recognizing this as a Bible verse, she thought those words must have been a line from a long-forgotten song.

Just before she left for her sister-in-law's house, she was interrupted by a phone call. This interruption was rather annoying, as it was delaying her departure. The caller identified herself as Lydia, a member of Katherine's congregation. Katherine vaguely could put a face to the name. Lydia was inviting Katherine to a weekly Bible Study class. Katherine quickly made excuses and told Lydia she was about to leave the house.

Katherine thought that would be the end of it, but little did she know. God had a different idea. Katherine left for her sister-in-law's and enjoyed the conversation, as usual. Returning home, Katherine found a note card stuck in the front door. It was from Lydia, who had called her earlier. The note revealed that Lydia had sensed something in their brief phone conversation that prompted her to pray for Katherine. She wanted to share some encouraging Bible verses with Katherine and included them in the note card.

The phone call and note card triggered a spiritual awakening for Katherine. Lydia became her spiritual guide, her confidant, her teacher, and her Christian friend. Katherine started studying God's Word with Lydia on a weekly basis. She came to Katherine's house for about an hour before leading a Bible study for the church group. Lydia held Katherine accountable as they studied God's Word together.

Yes, Katherine had been nudged by that note card from Lydia. The nudge was God calling her back to him. God knew that Katherine needed to mature in her faith. God was going to prepare her for future tasks and challenges. He had so much more to teach her. He had plans for her. In order to accomplish those plans, he needed Katherine back in his house and back in his Word. God nudged her. God knows how to reach each one of us. What moves one person may not get the attention of another. He knew what would work with Katherine.

How did Katherine know this nudge was from God? How did she know that God had connected her to Lydia? The front of the note card Lydia had left for her that day had a pretty picture of some flowers and the words, "Today is God's Gift!" The Bible verse boldly displayed on the front of the note card read, "This is the day the Lord has made; let us rejoice and be glad in it." The song in Katherine's head that morning and the Bible verse on the note card from Lydia were identical! To that, Katherine rejoiced and was glad. God had captured her full attention.

⌘

This is the day the LORD has made.
Let us rejoice and be glad in it.

Psalm 118:24 EHV

⌘

Pause to Ponder

There are times when God does something unique to get our attention. It may speak to us in a special way. It moves us. While others may say these things are just a coincidence, we know that God has had a hand in them. We are special to God, and he has his way of letting us know. In a world full of so many other people, he comes to us individually and touches our hearts in unmistakable ways.

Pause for Prayer

Dear Lord,

Thank you for this beautiful day. This day that you have made. Thank you for seeing me apart from all of your other children. Thank you for caring enough to let me know how much you care. Thank you for inviting me to have a personal relationship with you. Let me never take that for granted.

In Jesus's name.
Amen.

CHAPTER 20

Love, Allison

When God has done something amazing for you, what do you do with that? Do you shout it from the rooftops? Do you selfishly hoard your special experience all to yourself? And what do people think when you share that experience with them? Do they think you've gone off the deep end? Do they think you are a religious fanatic? Are they cautiously curious? Or, are they in awe and thinking, "I want some of that"? These are the kinds of reactions we can encounter when we share our faith with the world. When we share our faith with our family, it can get even more interesting. Even those who are brought up as Christians can wander from those roots.

Sometimes, as much as you try to hide from God and run from God, he pursues you. And, the truth is, we can't run fast enough or hide well enough to avoid him. Why would we even want to do that? Oh, we can have plenty of excuses and we can get very creative with those excuses. But…he knows. He knows what's in our hearts. And he has claimed us to be his. Just think of that. Despite our sinful nature, despite all the "better" Christians out there in the world, he wants us! Don't question why. Just be thankful!

You know how this goes. There is no one like you in the whole world. God knows that. He made you who you are. He gave you the talents and gifts you have. He has missions for you. Some missions that no one else but you can do in the way that you would do those missions. He has people in your circle or that you will meet that he wants you to bring to him or help get back on track. If those people see a change in you, your testimony will have a much bigger impact on their acceptance of him.

That takes us to Allison. She was experiencing an awakening in her faith. God was calling her back. She knew her brother, Joe, needed some of this too. She was concerned about his spiritual well-being. It seemed that both she and Joe had walked away from God even though they had been raised in a Christian home and had attended Christian elementary school. The clearer Allison's path became, the more she understood this journey didn't stop with her. God nudged her. He showed her that she was not supposed to hide his light under a bushel. She was ready to unveil the light. She had a lot to tell her brother. When someone senses a change in you, there might be some questions. Questions that need to be answered.

But in your hearts honor Christ the Lord as holy,
always being prepared to make a defense to anyone who
asks you for a reason for the hope that is in you;
yet do it with gentleness and respect.

1 Peter 3:15

Allison was nudged by God to write a letter to her brother, Joe, who lived some distance away. In simple, everyday conversational language she let her light shine. She pulled back the curtain on how her life had changed. It was raw. It was real. No-holds-barred. It was so honest it was gut-wrenching.

As Allison wrote to her brother, she quickly got past the opening niceties and drove full speed ahead to the gist of her letter. Let's look over Joe's shoulder as he reads part of the letter Allison sent him:

So what changed me? I'll admit my intentions were sometimes less than honorable at first. Pastor Miller was gone and we got a new pastor...my age, at that! Well, Mom would be happy to see me in church once in a while, so why not start over fresh with a new pastor? Okay, now I'm going to church...the strange thing is that this new pastor talks to the congregation, and not just at them. There are 200 plus people at the service, but why does he seem to be talking directly to me? While this feeling is new and a little uncomfortable sometimes, I find that I'm really listening to the sermons.

Before long, the pastor has announced a Bible study class open to all members of St Paul's and prospective new members. Well, that's not for me. After all I went to the Lutheran school for nine years and besides, I bowl on Thursday evenings. However the response to the class is overwhelming. More than 70 people signed up for a 16-week class. Don't they have anything better to do?

Now Mom invites me to the Ladies Aid Christmas luncheon. How can I say "no" when she already knows that I don't have any kids to watch that day? I shouldn't have opened my big mouth! Oh well, it's a free meal and I don't have to worry about being talked into joining Ladies Aid because I do usually babysit on Wednesday afternoons. After all, Ladies Aid is for old, retired ladies with nothing better to do. Oh, oh…now Mrs. Campbell (Chairman of the Altar Guild for the last hundred years or so) wants to talk to me. Will I do what? Serve on the Altar Guild with her and another lady for the Sundays in March? Well, that doesn't sound too difficult… besides, she looks like she expects me to say "no" so I'll shock her and say "yes". Boy, what have I gotten myself into? Now I'll be expected to be in church on each one of those Sundays in March!

As if that isn't enough, Pastor Wright is standing here saying how pleased he is with the turnout for his Bible study class. I figure that he knows that I'm not one of those attending, so I tell him that I would have liked to have come, but Thursday is my bowling night. I found out later how that would come back to haunt me. In the spring, he repeated the same class with choices of Monday morning or Tuesday evening. Well, I'd better choose one and get it over with. At least this pastor is a good speaker so the class shouldn't be boring.

It turns out that the class is not boring, in fact, it's quite interesting. Does the Bible really say all those things? What else am I going to discover in there? Now, I find that Bible study is kind of like opening a bag of potato chips…I'm beginning to want more! This is definitely a new feeling. Is it my imagination or am I also actually looking forward to going to church on Sundays?

What is this new eagerness to learn? I thought I already knew it all...maybe I can really take what I learn and apply it to my life. Pastor Wright says it works. Of course, he would believe it! That's why he's a pastor. Okay – he showed us all kinds of places in the Bible about "how much" and "when" and "with what attitude" we should give money to the church. He talks about giving of our time and talents, too, but everyone knows that the church is really interested in our treasures. I guess I felt guilty that I spent more at the bowling alley than I put in the church plate. So I will make an effort to change how much I give to church. It's a long story but I find out that Pastor Wright was right! Just when I think I'm going to be broke all week if I put that money in the church envelope, something happens, and I'm not. I share this biblical information of "giving" with my husband, and his attitude seems to change toward giving to his church, too. Hmmm, amazing...

Now we're talking about building a new house. This is scary! We can hardly make it from pay check to pay check and make a house payment of $114 a month as it is. Maybe I'd better pray for a sign of some sort – maybe we could win that magazine sweepstakes! Plans are shaping up to sell our old house and build this new one. Why did I cut the picture of this new house out of the Sunday paper that day anyway? Did I really think that we would build it someday?

Now one "coincidence" after another lets everything fall into place for us. Is this really happening? Even Mike *agrees that this is a little too good to be true. Do we dare believe that God has a hand in this? It sounds a little corny, but what other explanation is there? We're not special – we certainly don't deserve this – but does God actively work and intervene in our daily lives? Aren't we supposed to just believe in God, spend an hour in church on Sunday mornings (when it's convenient for us) and hope there's really a heaven to go to after we've lived a full life and died at the ripe old age of 98 years. You mean there's more? We're supposed to live our faith? Put our trust in God for everything in life and not just "in case of emergencies". What! Pray too? Sure, I can recite the Lord's Prayer and say "now I lay me down to sleep…" but Pastor Wright says prayer is talking to God like a kid talks to a parent. Prayer is from the heart – and personal, not recited. I suppose next, I'm supposed to be convinced that God answers all prayers. Well, when we got that unexpected bill just before Christmas for $250 more than the estimate, I prayed! I prayed that we would win the $250 in the state lottery "Match 3" Game. I wasn't being greedy – I only prayed for the amount we needed – no more…no less. Guess what, we didn't win. We were still sweating about how to pay the bill. Sure, it helped that the guy knocked $100 off the bill because he had been so far off on the original labor estimate. And it didn't hurt that Mom gave us $100 for a Christmas present. That final $50 wasn't quite so hard to come up with. But still, God didn't answer my prayer…or did he?*

Now tell me, does this really sound like a religious fanatic to you? Nowhere did you hear about a burning bush, a voice in a dream, or a mysterious vision. I haven't been brainwashed. I'm not wrapped up in some passing fad. My faith was on hold. It was slowly awakened from its dormant stage, nurtured by the Word of God, and has been growing ever since. That's just the beginning of what's been happening in my life. I see the hand of the Lord working in my life every day. I'm learning what he expects of me. So now, when I write to you with an apparent obsession with religion, it's because, from what I've learned, I'm concerned for you.

Love,
Your Sister, Allison

This letter was not something a brother could very easily ignore. Maybe this mission wasn't going to end with one letter, but Allison was going to try. She was going to do her part. Her light was shining brightly. She put it on its stand and let it shine on her brother. She knew God would take over from there.

Thirty years after writing the letter to her brother, Allison still has a copy of it in her Bible. She doesn't know why she saved a copy. Whatever the reason, it serves as a beautiful reminder to Allison of where she was in her faith at that time, how she was thinking, and why she lives life as she does today.

❧

"You are the light of the world.
A town built on a hill cannot be hidden.
Neither do people light a lamp and put it under a bowl.

Instead they put it on its stand,
and it gives light to everyone in the house.
In the same way, let your light shine before others,
that they may see your good deeds
and glorify your Father in heaven.

Matthew 5:14-16 NIV

Pause to Ponder

Sharing our faith is not always easy. We put ourselves out there and are subjected to different reactions. Some think we're fanatics. Some think we are crazy. Some avoid us. We have concerns about loved ones and their eternal future.

All we can do is follow God's nudges. We can help plant the seed and let God take over from there. We can share what our faith means to us. The biggest statement we can make is by showing others the difference that God makes through how we live our lives. Have they noticed changes in us? Do they see more peace? Would they like to have that in their life? We can try to anticipate their questions and be ready with some answers and God's Word. Be honest. Keep it real. That's what we need to do.

Pause for Prayer

Dear Lord,

We long to have all of our friends and relatives know you. We often feel inadequate to share you with others. We often lack the courage to talk to others. We ask that you give us the right approach and the right words to help move them. Send your Holy Spirit to touch their hearts to want to know you better. Nudge them to learn more about you. Encourage them to pick up the Bible and study your Word. Thank you for caring for our eternal welfare. Thank you for sending Jesus to do what only he could do for us. Praise be to you, Lord.

In Jesus's name.
Amen.

CHAPTER 21

Danger in Morocco

It was 1986. Janet's husband was in the Army and stationed in Schweinfurt, Germany. Since he had an accompanied tour, Janet and her daughter were able to live there with him. Janet was young and adventurous. She was fascinated by this different land. She felt a yearning to travel to Morocco before her husband was relocated back to the States.

Morocco, an Arabian country, is about twenty miles from Spain. They are separated by the Strait of Gibraltar. Janet was curious about it. She had told her husband that she wanted to go tour Morocco, and he wasn't overly receptive to the idea. Knowing his wife as he did, he knew he could not talk her out of it.

Her plan was to ride the train to Morocco all by herself. Janet's husband was still very apprehensive about letting her take this trip. Janet had not read or researched about the country prior to her departure. She really was not prepared for what lay ahead of her. As

Janet prepared to step onto the train, her husband said, "You better come back. I have too much of value on this train." He was talking about her. She was of great value to him. Janet had a warm feeling to know that he cared so much about her.

As the train pulled away, Janet thought about the changes in her life. She was a long way from the small Midwest farm she grew up on. She was always up for seeing the world, even if she had to do it by herself. She was not going to be denied of this opportunity.

The train pulled into Portbou, Spain, a small town in the middle of the mountains and on the border of Spain and France. It was there that she met a girl named Piper. Piper was leaving her friends behind to also travel to Morocco alone. Piper was from Boston and blessed to be fluent in French, Spanish, and Japanese. As Janet and Piper got acquainted, they decided to travel together to Morocco.

Janet and Piper traveled down the coast of Spain. They loved wine and enjoyed the good Sangria. As they spent time together, Janet and Piper developed a friendship. Piper affectionately called Janet the crazy blonde lady. They traveled to Algeciras, Spain, while trying to find a way to Tangier, Morocco. When they reached Morocco, they noticed an immediate change in their environment. They soon saw indications of hatred for Americans on display. Burning dummies depicting President Reagan were hanging from buildings. There was also talk of the Libyan President Gaddafi being up to something with chemicals.

Things were getting scary and the women were feeling vulnerable in this foreign land. Instead of traveling to Tangier, Morocco, as originally planned, they decided to board a ferry to Ceuta, Morocco, and walk across the border. There they met a young Japanese man who was traveling from South America to return to Japan. The three of them talked about their plans and decided to walk together to the next town.

As the three of them made their plans, the locals in Morocco had other ideas. They kept trying to talk them into taking a taxi. Finally, the threesome agreed and took the taxi. It cost them fifty cents to travel twenty miles to the town of Tetouan.

The two men driving the taxi pulled into a village, stopped, and said they had to get gas. In reality, they weren't stopping for gas at all. The two men stood by the windows of the car to block the view of Piper, Janet, and the Japanese man. They opened the trunk and threw something in. In alarm, Piper said to Janet, "I think they are using us to smuggle in hash!" Hash is the slang word for hashish, which is known for its intoxicating effect. Piper had done some reading and research about Morocco before the trip, whereas Janet had not. Janet had no idea what a dangerous situation they were getting into.

As the two taxi drivers got back in the car, Janet and Piper asked the men about getting gas, but they were met with a stern command to be quiet. The cab got back on the highway with the three foreigners. There were checkpoints throughout the country. When the cab had to stop at the checkpoint, the police looked them over. The cab driver asked them where their passports were. Janet and Piper did not feel comfortable giving up their passports in a country as scary as Morocco. They finally had to cooperate and hand over their passports. Meanwhile, the cab driver gave the police a bribe so they would not look in the trunk.

Piper and Janet decided to get out of the taxi at the next city, but the Moroccans had a different plan. They blocked the doors and windows from their view until they were able to remove the mysterious items from the trunk.

Later that night, many Moroccans were smoking hash. It appeared that Piper had been right. Hash is a drug made from compressing and then processing part of the hemp plant. It is usually consumed orally or by smoking in a pipe. The penalty for trafficking hash was prison time.

Piper, Janet, and the Japanese man traveled throughout Morocco for nine days using the local buses. In Casablanca, when the lights were off inside the bus, Janet was groped by an off-duty policeman. She rammed him in the ribs until he yelped. Suddenly, the lights came on, and he then behaved himself. When Janet and Piper got to Marrakesh, they got off the bus. But the off-duty policeman was not going to give up easily. He wanted to stay with Janet. Finally, Janet and Piper had to chase him back onto the bus.

When Janet and Piper got to Tangier, more danger was waiting for them. Some men wanted to take Janet and Piper to a hotel. When the women refused to go with them, the men beat up Piper. The men had an evil motive. The men wanted to take the women to the motel so they could get a commission. Eventually, the women found a policeman to ask for help. When he heard what was going on, he told the women to get a different tour guide.

Janet and Piper ended up living on the beach for a few days at Agadir. They stayed with the blue people. The blue people wear indigo gowns and handle camels. One night, Janet and Piper dressed up and went to a disco. Janet decided to participate in the local culture. She dressed up in the long gown that the Moroccan women wore. When she entered the disco, it seemed she was the only person dressed like that. She later learned that the unmarried Moroccans wore Western clothes until they were married.

Janet learned many things from all that happened on that trip. There was the lack of forethought about the trip. There was danger and fear during the situations encountered.

Having grown up on a farm and living a fairly sheltered life, Janet had a fast and rude awakening to the realities of life in a foreign country. She could picture the story of her life showing in a movie theater. The marquee would read, "Farm Girl Meets the World."

Janet firmly believes she and Piper could have been imprisoned when they were used to smuggle in hash. She feels God was teaching her to be more careful. Since then, Janet has been on many trips to foreign lands, but she now uses tours that have been deemed safe and does her homework before she travels.

God revealed his power and protection to her throughout her travels. He nudged her with an appreciation for his protection and care despite her lack of preparation for the trip and her questionable decisions about the trip. She shudders to think of what might have happened had she and Piper not gotten away from the evil men who were on the bus. She acknowledges that without God's intervention and protection, the trip could have ended much differently for herself and the other two travelers.

Years later, Janet wonders what God thought as he looked at all this. She thinks he would have said, "This girl needs watching. I have to watch out for fools."

Janet knows that despite the dangers in this world, the Lord is always with her. She has the best travel companion anyone could have. With him at her side, she can be strong. She can be courageous regardless of what the trip brings her way.

She marvels at how God brought her together with two English-speaking strangers in a foreign country. She is amazed that God led her to Piper and the young Japanese man so that they could help each other through some of the frightening ordeals they encountered. What started as two female strangers in a foreign land ended up in a very close friendship. She also gives thanks to God and gives him all the credit for protecting them and keeping them safe in a very dangerous situation.

Where Janet lacked the linguistics and pre-trip research, Piper offered that knowledge to the group. Janet, Piper, and the Japanese man thought they were traveling together as a threesome. Janet later realized there were actually four of them traveling together. You see,

God was right there with them the entire time. Keeping them safe. Protecting them. Wherever they went. Whatever they encountered.

∽

Have I not commanded you?
Be strong and courageous.
Do not be afraid; do not be discouraged,
for the Lord your God will be with you wherever you go.

Joshua 1:9 NIV

∽

Pause to Ponder

In their travels, Janet and Piper had endured several harrowing situations. Time after time, God rescued them. In the excitement of the travels and the fear from the ongoing situations, the reality of it all didn't fully register with Janet until it was all over and she had time to think about it. Time after time, God's protection was with them. This trip could have ended badly. Very badly. How often do we put ourselves in harm's way? As we make decisions in life, we have a counselor to help us. We can call on him to help us make good decisions. Even then, we may sometimes face frightening situations. As we do, we can call out to the Lord to help us and save us. As he comes to our rescue, may we lift our voices in thanksgiving and praise for his almighty protection.

Pause for Prayer

Dear Lord,

We come to you with thankful hearts. You are always there for us. Even when we are not totally aware, you are guarding, protecting, and rescuing us from danger and evil. What comfort it is to know how much you care for each of us. Please let us never take your protection for granted. Help us to remember to lean on you as we face fear and danger. In those frightening moments in life, please give us your peace and protection.

In Jesus's name.
Amen.

CHAPTER 22

Delivered from Depression

Troubles! The world is full of troubles. Living in this sin-filled world, we can't expect everything to be perfect. As Christians, we know we will have hardships. But sometimes, despite knowing that, we can reach a point where it can feel as though there are just too many hardships to bear. The burdens and the worries can pile on top of each other and leave us struggling to cope. Yes, we often let our hearts be troubled.

Violet is a sweet woman. She led a busy life between doing things with her family and friends. She was blessed with children and grandchildren who loved her dearly. She was involved. Even though she was a senior citizen, she kept busy. She would watch her grandchildren some days and take friends to the city other days to shop for supplies. She had a health challenge of diabetes. As she progressed through her senior years, she had experienced a few "incidents" while behind the wheel that caused her a little concern. She thought it best to not say anything to her children about that at this time. She was afraid they might want her to give up driving.

Aging isn't easy. It involves change…a lot of change. And many of the changes are not what we want.

Little did Violet know that the challenges were only beginning. Challenges, not only for her but for her entire family. Her son was diagnosed with cancer. He is a big strong-looking guy resembling his father, who had passed away many years before. Her son's family already had challenges to deal with, and now this. Violet watched as her son dealt with the pain of a vertebrae crushed by a tumor. Her son began radiation treatments. Violet was relieved that her son's cancer responded to the treatments. The challenges were not over, however. In time, he was diagnosed with a tumor near the base of one of the bones in his hand. That resulted in a broken bone in his hand. Violet's heart was troubled.

The family challenges continued. One of Violet's daughters was also diagnosed with cancer. This time it was colon cancer. Her daughter began chemo treatments while her son was going through radiation treatments.

It is hard for a mother to deal with illness in her children at any age, but to watch two of your adult children endure treatments to fight cancer simultaneously is more than difficult. Violet's heart was feeling anxious.

Meanwhile, it was time for Violet's annual checkup. Imagine receiving the call that she needed to return to the clinic after her mammogram results were read by the doctor. And then, there it was…a third cancer diagnosis for this family. The cancer was contained in Violet's milk duct, and the doctors recommended doing a lumpectomy (which removes the lump only), followed by radiation. Violet's daughter intervened. Acting as an advocate for her mother, she researched and determined this to not be a good option for her mother at her age. Violet's daughter thought it best for Violet to do the lumpectomy only and opt out of the offer of radiation treatment. Violet went ahead with the surgery and declined the radiation treatments. By now, Violet was feeling the weight of her troubled heart.

Things started changing after that. Violet experienced a quick decline into depression and confusion. The family thought it best that Violet enter a local nursing home for care. She appeared to be having a nervous breakdown. She was not happy about coming to the nursing home. She was depressed. She stayed in bed and cried. She didn't want to talk to anyone. She would face the wall and not even acknowledge her own kids when they came to see her. The pastor visited her. The family minister gave her communion. She felt like she was losing her faith. At one point, Violet didn't even feel like attending the family Thanksgiving. It had all become too much for her to bear.

Due to the depression, Violet was prescribed medications to help with that. Often, it can take time and patience to get medications for depression right for each individual. This was a challenge in Violet's case, as well. The medications played mind games with her. At one point, Violet was convinced that there were kittens in her closet at the nursing home. Another day, she thought her pastor had used his foot to push the kittens away. Later, she thought one of the ladies who visited her had taken the kittens home to care for them. Her daughters had Yorkies. Violet also thought she was responsible for caring for them during this time of confusion.

Violet had always been close with her granddaughter, but now even her granddaughter, Summer, said she didn't know what to do for her. Violet's son told Summer to pray with her. Summer did just that. And Summer noticed something…when she started praying with her grandmother, Violet started relaxing. Yes, God was there… providing comfort during a difficult time.

Meanwhile, things were happening at the nursing home. When Violet was moved into the nursing home, she had to take a less-than-desirable room. Her room was in an old wing of the nursing home. It had cement block walls that were painted white. One past resident had described that same room as looking like a white-washed barn when she had been living in it. Here was a lady already in a state of depression, living in a depressing room. This was not a good situation;

however, moving her to another room could also be risky. Sometimes, changes are upsetting to residents. Moving Violet to another floor would mean different caregivers, as well. This could also cause distress to a resident. The family didn't have to be concerned about it, though, as God was at work in many ways. Yes, God had a plan.

Soon they were notified that Violet was going to be temporarily moved to another room while the nursing home did maintenance on her current room. The good news was that the temporary room was more modern and cheery looking. The bad news was that the move might cause even more depression and confusion. At first Violet didn't want to stay in the new room. Her daughter thought the nicer room was a positive for her mother, so she arranged for her mother to stay in there on a permanent basis.

When Violet needed it most, God sent loving caregivers to help her along. As Violet's nurse made the rounds, she would say to her, "You know what I need," as she opened her arms wide. She made Violet stand up and give her a hug.

God wasn't done with Violet yet. The family minister from Violet's church started a Bible class in the complex where the nursing home was located. This enabled people from the nursing home, the assisted living apartments, and others living in the complex to attend Bible classes. What a blessing this class turned out to be! The Bible class, which was customized to a senior population, was helping Violet adjust and accept her life changes. Bible class attendees came to visit Violet. One of the Bible class ladies came to get her in her wheelchair and took her to chapel. Becky (a different Bible class leader) kept coming to visit Violet. One day, Becky started humming Violet a hymn. Violet told her to be quiet. "I don't need to hear that," she said. But Becky didn't let that stop her. Violet's loved ones, friends, and church members were not going to give up on her. God wasn't going to either. God knew what Violet needed. Time after time, he gave her little nudges, reminding her that he was there for her.

Within four months of entering the nursing home, Violet had a much better outlook on life. After the worst of times were over, Violet recognized the Lord's hand in all that she had endured and overcome with his help. She credits the nursing home Bible class, reading the Bible and devotions, and watching the *Time of Grace* television broadcast with helping her get back on track. She recognized that she was being nudged to return to her faith and restore her hope in the Lord.

It seems God had just the right prescription all along. All Violet needed was the right dosage of her Savior's Word, mixed with reminders of his love and forgiveness, plus love and care from family and friends, Christian fellowship, and daily hugs from a nurse.

God has a never-ending pile of prescription sheets. Even though what ails us may vary, each prescription looks the same. Among other things, that prescription covers troubled hearts. We have unlimited refills available of his Word, his forgiveness, and his love. Every fill of those prescriptions is available to us for free, thanks to Jesus. All we have to do is follow his dosage instructions. When we take his prescription as directed, it becomes much easier to add self-care and love for others to our regimen. As we remove the anxiety from our troubled hearts, God fills the void with his indescribable peace.

Peace I leave with you; my peace I give you.
I do not give to you as the world gives.
Do not let your hearts be troubled and do not be afraid.

John 14:27 NIV

Pause to Ponder

Depression and anxiety have become very common. It is serious, but it is treatable. The number of people taking anti-depressants is staggering. Life can become unbearable for some suffering from depression. The pressures of life, the challenges, and the sad things happening, one after another, all add to this problem. For some, it seems they get dealt more than their fair share of concerns to be anxious over. As the burdens of life weigh one down, depression takes hold. It is then that we need reminders of where our hope lies. The burdens of this world are real, but they are temporary. Unfortunately, as we deal with them, they can feel like they are going on forever. For believers, this is an opportunity to lift up others. For the depressed, it is an opportunity to cling to their faith with hope and trust. Where fear and anxiety are building, God's hope and peace can come storming in to knock it out. What a blessing that God rescues us from the torment of depression!

Pause for Prayer

Dear Lord,

Sometimes we feel so anxious. At times, the troubles in this world can weigh us down. When we face those anxious times, remind us to come to you. Nudge us to remember you are here to help us with those fears, cares, and burdens. Strengthen us with your Word and the assurance of your love and care for us. When we see others struggling to get through anxious times, help us be there for them and encourage them through your Word.

In Jesus's name.
Amen.

CHAPTER 23

It Could Have Been Me

God was at work on Natalie's heart. She had been going through a lot in her personal life. Yet she was learning and growing in her faith. She had been involved in a children's ministry, then later a Christian recovery group.

Now, God was moving her once again. For about a year a woman from her church had been inviting Natalie to join a women's prison ministry group that is found all over the world. As she prayed, the Lord worked on her heart. She felt him nudging her to get involved in this group. Because of Natalie's shy personality, this would not be an easy decision.

It was a busy and difficult time in her life. She was busy packing up her parents for a long move back to their original area to be near family as aging set in. She was starting work at a new job in a school system. She was also going through a divorce.

Despite all that was going on in her life, the Lord kept working on her heart. After about a year, Natalie decided to take part in the prison ministry group. She knew this would be a challenge for her, as she is an introvert, but she knew she had to follow God's lead on this.

Natalie was broken as she went to visit the prison, but she was determined to reach out and help others. The Lord was leading her to look beyond herself. The group of three outside women went in to be with six inmates for four days. Local churches put the visiting women up for the night and fed them.

As Natalie got involved with the prison ministry, she felt she was doing this to help the Lord. In reality, as she looks back, she feels the Lord was really helping her.

The program was quite structured. They had talks and a forgiveness ceremony. The prison women were giving it to the Lord and getting prayed over. In the gym, the ministry leaders would decorate the tables differently each day at the prison. The servant girls (inmates who were past graduates of the program) cleaned up afterward.

Each group had different personalities and different dynamics. One of the prisoners, named Anna, was rather quiet and hung back. The food and treats they brought to the meetings were a big attraction for her. The prisoners were not allowed to keep extra food that they did not consume at the meetings. As it came time to clean up, the servant girls took away the extra food.

Do you remember eating those twin packs of yellow sponge cake with the fluffy white filling? Anna remembered them. She loved them. They were so good and they were among the treasured treats that were whisked away. Anna became upset that they took the extra food away.

They went to the chapel, where the prisoners saw a table covered in a tablecloth. They pulled back the tablecloth to reveal wooden crosses to give to each of the participants. Natalie knew that Anna was upset about losing out on the sponge cakes. She said to Anna, "Sometimes God takes something away and gives us something better."

Part of the goal of the program is to create God Gangs. The God Gangs were a family within the prison. What a perfect term to use with a prison population. They try to teach the prisoners to rely on each other. They also were given a chance to go before the group and give a testimony. Anna, shy as she was, eventually went up to talk. "They offered me a cream-filled sponge cake to come up," she said. Food is indeed a powerful motivator. Surely, God has a sense of humor too!

The women's ministry group members would write 42 cards for each inmate. They would also ask seven friends to write seven cards. On the third day of the program, the girls went into the makeshift church. The servers set up the tables and put a bag of cards at each place. The prisoner participants sat in their chairs and read the cards while the prison ministry leaders sang. Some of the inmates never received mail. There was never a dry eye in the building during this time. It was very moving to them to know that someone else was thinking of them and cared.

The ministry group also did an angel tree to solicit gifts for the inmates prior to Christmas. Later, they would deliver the gifts at Christmas time.

At one point, the governor was activating a program to release many prisoners from their state back into society. As they implemented this program, the potential release candidates were interviewed. A prisoner named Laverne was interviewed for this program. She was asked, "Why should we release you?" Amazingly honest, Laverne said, "I shouldn't be released. I took a man's life." Natalie couldn't help but wonder about this. Would Laverne have recognized that without the women's ministry program?

Natalie originally didn't think participating in this program was a good fit for her, but she is glad she did it. They have monthly meetings. She participates in this three day in-prison program about once a year. Natalie grew from this program by learning to give speeches and give her testimony. She spent six hours working on her speech and she delivered it well. It was a breakthrough moment for her.

More and more requirements seem to be complicating the program. Now they have to apply, get approved, and be fingerprinted to participate. Natalie has found that as you try to do these things to serve the Lord, you have to sometimes be working against Satan to get in there and accomplish the task.

The biggest blessing and takeaway that Natalie has had from the program is self-realization. We are all sinners. None of us are perfect. None of us are immune. Those behind bars made a bad choice. Sometimes, they made that bad choice in a split second. For those of us walking free, any one of us could slip, make a poor decision, lose our temper, and, in a nanosecond, be caught up in a situation that could land us in prison. Natalie was humbled. She learned to love more.

Natalie thought, "I am no better than them." One wrong choice is all that separates any one of us from being locked in those cells and longing for cream-filled sponge cake. When people have lived a life with dysfunctional relationships and addictions, it would not have taken much to give in to anger and end up in this situation. Natalie is aware of how fragile these situations are. "It could have been me," she says.

God nudged Natalie. He moved her. She hesitated, but he kept this calling in front of her. She sought to be faithful to the Lord with her service to the imprisoned women. As she did so, God helped her with an important life lesson. Each experience, each bit of growth, each painful ordeal, each light bulb moment…they are all stepping stones. And God is there holding our hand to keep us steady. He softens our hearts with compassion. He helps us look beyond ourselves and our own life challenges. He guides our feet over the slippery stones lest we slip and fall. This slippery walk through life would be so very difficult without him.

When did we see you sick or in prison and go to visit you?'
"The King will reply, 'Truly I tell you,
whatever you did for one of the least
of these brothers and sisters of mine, you did for me.'

Matthew 25:39-40 NIV

Pause to Ponder

How often do we think about the imprisoned? How often do we pray for them? Do we judge them and think we are better than them? We do not know their stories. We do not know what has influenced their lives and led to the poor choices they have made. One thing we do know...they are all God's children. God loves them. He loves them just as much as he loves you and me. Knowing that, is there anything we can do to humble ourselves and support them? Is there a way we can lift them up and bring them the good news that they so desperately need to turn their lives around? If we can't support them directly, what can we do to support and encourage those who do?

Pause for Prayer

Dear Lord,

We live our lives in our comfortable homes and doing as we please. We go where we want when we want. We thank you for those freedoms. We often tend to judge and look down on those who are outcast and imprisoned. Some of them are good people who slipped. Some of them are repentant. Some of them never had much of a chance at life because of a rough start. We ask you to touch their hearts and bring them close to you. Teach them about repentance. Let them experience your love and forgiveness. Teach them of our Savior. We also ask that you nudge others to minister to them and teach them of your ways. Please give us forgiving and compassionate hearts.

In Jesus's name.
Amen.

CHAPTER 24

Miracle on the Mountain

Her mom had something to tell her. It wasn't an easy story to tell. In fact, she had never told anyone this story. Seven years earlier, something had happened. Amy sat face-to-face with her mom, waiting and listening. She could tell this was something very emotional that her mom had kept private.

Amy's mom, Julia, had faced plenty of challenges in life. In 1972, when Amy was 19 years old, her father died in an industrial accident. Grief is hard for any family. Being a young family doesn't help. Amy's brother was 30. Her two sisters were 26 and 21. Her mom was 52. Amy married and started raising her own family.

In time, Julia started trying to get back to a somewhat normal life. She started going to dances with her girlfriends. At one of the dances, she met Ray. He was a very good dancer. They enjoyed dancing together that evening and soon started dating and going to dances together. Dances provided a lot of enjoyment for them. They even entered and won contests for being the best dancers.

After suffering through the grieving process, Julia was thrilled to have found someone that she could have so much fun with. Time passed and they continued to date. Life was good. Eventually Ray and Julia got married.

Although she thought her life had taken a turn for the better, Julia was in for a surprise. The day after their wedding, Ray started showing a different personality. He changed into an abuser. He would threaten Julia. He hit Julia. It made no difference what she did; the abuse became a regular part of their life. When Amy and her siblings would visit their mom, they would find her covered in bruises. Ray even broke her glasses when he was beating her. Fear and anguish became a part of daily life for Julia.

Amy's mom worked at a nursing home as a nursing assistant. She was used to taking care of herself financially, as Ray never contributed to the finances. Julia believed that since she had married Ray, she should stay with him. She thought he would change. Her faith and her determination made it apparent to her that she should try to help Ray with his problems. She had no plans to leave him.

It was a mystery as to why Ray had these dramatic moods. In time, Julia learned that Ray had obtained a brain injury from fighting in the war. She wondered if this had something to do with his outbursts of temper and abuse.

Julia had a strong faith. She had always prayed a lot in the past and now was no exception. She asked God to help keep her safe from the terror she was now living in with her second husband.

To escape the worst of Midwest winters, Julia and Ray went to Arizona every winter. Amy already knew all this. But now, Amy's mom was about to reveal something that she had never shared before.

Four years into their marriage, Ray told Julia that on this trip to Arizona, he wanted to take her to see the Superstition Mountains, which are located about an hour's drive east of Phoenix, Arizona. The Superstitions, as they are called, are a local favorite recreation activity. This desert mountain range has many hiking trails varying in levels of difficulty. Accounts vary but indicate that the Superstition Mountains reach a maximum elevation of just over 3,600 to 5,000 feet. Consisting of jagged cliffs and deep canyons, the Superstitions have a reputation for being a rough territory. Many vehicles had plunged over the edge of the road over the years. Unverified tales abound of a large number of mysterious deaths occurring there. The Superstitions are said to have taken the lives of over 600 people in the last one hundred years. Just hearing the name of the mountains invoked a spark of curiosity.

Ray drove up the Superstition Mountains. As they neared the top, he pulled over to stop at a very high lookout point. Ray told Julia to get out of the car and get closer so she could see the view better. There were no barriers at that time. Julia was standing close to the edge. She was about three feet from the drop-off of the lookout point when Ray approached her from behind. He put his hands on her arms and started pushing. Ray was trying to push her over the edge! Terror flooded over Julia. She knew at that moment that she was just a couple of seconds from being pushed to her death. Her husband wanted to kill her! Julia's deep faith took over. She turned to her best and only help in such an impossible situation. "God, help me!" she shouted.

That's when it happened. At that very moment, a man wearing a white robe appeared. Imagine the surprise. Think of how breathtaking this would be. She and Ray both saw him. And then, the man in the white robe spoke. He stated in a loud, authoritative voice, "Go back to the car!" Ray immediately stopped pushing her. He took his hands off of her. Julia said that they were no longer in control of the situation. Ray was unable to do anything other than obey the command of the man in the white robe. Ray and Julia both walked back to the car. As she was walking, Julia looked back for another glimpse of the man in the white robe, but he was gone. Ray and Julia drove down the mountain and back home in silence, never speaking of the incident.

Time passed and Ray and Julia had still never discussed the incident. One can only imagine the awe that Julia felt knowing that God had saved her life in an instant that day. Ray and Julia continued to live under the same roof. Unfortunately, Ray did not change. The abuse continued. Julia was diagnosed with cancer. She underwent grueling treatments. The time came for the annual trip to Arizona for the winter. Julia just wasn't up to it with the cancer and the treatments she was enduring. Imagine the fear she must have felt to be so weak and ill while living under these stressful conditions. Imagine the fear of going back to that horrible place after what she had endured there. Julia told Ray that she would stay home. Ray went anyway and was gone for several months as Julia stayed home alone dealing with the cancer treatments. She was not doing well. Ray never called in all that time to check on her. One day, at the end of winter, Ray called Julia. He told her he would be coming home the next day. Julia told Ray that when he got there, his packed suitcases would be on the front steps. She told him that this was the end of the marriage. Two years after the incident on Superstition Mountain, Julia divorced Ray.

It was about seven years later that Julia finally told her daughter what had happened that day in the Superstition Mountains. It was frightening to think of how things could have turned out that day. Ray had gone to the Superstitions with a plan. He no doubt knew that there were many tales of people mysteriously disappearing or dying in those jagged cliffs and deep canyons within the mountains. It certainly would have made getting away with murder a possibility.

Julia never had any doubts. Yes, she had been nudged by God. In her greatest hour of need, she put her full trust in God and called out to him. She knew that God had saved her life that day. As life continued, she thought about that moment. She believed that God was telling her to trust in him and that he would take care of her. She had no reason not to trust him. After all, he had saved her life in an instant on that mountain at the authoritative command of a man wearing a white robe.

~

In my distress I called to the LORD;
I cried to my God for help.
From his temple he heard my voice;
my cry came before him, into his ears.

Psalm 18:6 NIV

~

Pause to Ponder

Julia's experience was quite dramatic. One would have to take notice of such an event. Yet, God often does things for all of us throughout our lives to keep us safe. Some are subtle, and others are not. Some we notice. Some we don't. Are you watching, observing, and really paying attention to God's hand in your life? Are you giving credit where it is due when he does these things? Do you give thanks for all the times he has kept you safe from a potentially serious situation? Are you telling people about it? Or do you tuck the memory away, afraid to share with others the great things that he has done for you?

Pause for Prayer

Dear Lord,

Sometimes, we are fearful. Sometimes, we find ourselves in dangerous situations and feel helpless to save ourselves. Keep our faith strong. Help us to have that immediate response to call on you for help. Help us to recognize when you save us and protect us. We thank you for all the times you have saved us, protected us, and guarded us from danger. Give us the courage to share those things with others so that they, too, can see the mighty things that you do for us. We praise you for your loving attention and care.

In Jesus's name.
Amen.

CHAPTER 25

Finding Her Reason for Being

Many people never know. They may wonder. They may be curious. They may even feel driven to know, but many are not sure. It was very important to Amy. She needed to know her life's purpose. Even at a young age, she had been working on a relationship with God. She wanted to please him in every way. Yet, to feel like she was truly doing that, she needed to know why God had put her on this earth. She wanted to focus on that.

In 1956, Amy was just five years old. Her big sister, Nora, was six years old. Her sister was a gifted student. She had done so well that they were thinking of advancing her in school by skipping a grade.

For now, school was out, and the warm summer weather brought the rain and the flowers. It also brought out the mosquitoes. Suddenly, Nora was stricken with encephalitis. She ran a fever of 106 degrees and went into convulsions. After several days in the hospital, her fever finally broke. Relief for the family was short-lived. They soon learned that Nora's brain had been damaged to the point that she had lost all knowledge that she had acquired in her first six years. She didn't know her parents. She didn't know her siblings. She couldn't eat or talk. And now, she couldn't perform even basic functions in life.

The family brought Nora home and began the process of teaching her how to eat, how to talk, and all the basic functions in life. At that time, when she was only five years old, Amy's mother told Amy that she now needed to be the big sister and teach her sister everything she knew. At only five years old, Amy took this responsibility seriously. Her mom told her anytime she needed help to pray to God and he would help her. That is just what Amy did. In reality, at only five years old, her life became a life of prayer every day. She would pray for God's guidance and pray that he would heal her sister's brain. She did not realize at that tender age that caring for her sister would be a lifelong commitment.

Amy's young caregiver days didn't stop with just her sister. One Friday night, when Amy was nine years old, her twenty-year-old brother, Paul, was standing by the road and struck by a drunk driver.

Paul's leg was crushed in three places. He went into a coma for seven months. He sustained brain damage. The brain damage wasn't caused directly by the accident but rather by bone marrow from his crushed leg traveling to his brain. When he came out of the coma, he couldn't speak. He couldn't walk.

When Paul was able to be released from the hospital, they brought him home. Everyone in the household helped care for Paul. That included his little sister, Amy. They helped him in the bathroom, they fed him. When his widowed mother got remarried, her second husband did not want him kept at home. At that time, Paul was moved to a care facility.

Paul had a big heart. He had a strong faith in God. When he could finally speak a little, the family soon learned how forgiving he was. He was beat up in the care facility. He had no anger or bitterness about it. When the family would express anger over it, Paul would say, "Just forget it. Forgive him. It will be okay." Despite all the disabilities he had acquired and the struggle with day-to-day living,

Paul was an example for others. When people went to visit Paul, they saw a picture of Jesus hanging on the wall in his room. He always went to church when he was given the opportunity. He was clear on his purpose: to show compassion, even when in a bad situation.

Finally, after 58 years, Paul's body was giving up the struggle to live. Paul lay there as he stared and reached up. He pulled his hand back. Then he reached up again. He had a very focused stare for several days prior to his passing. Out of her brother's 58 years, Amy's brother was in a wheelchair for the last 38 years of his life. Once again, Amy had played the role of caregiver. Once again, God reminded her of her life's purpose.

At age 55, Amy had a strong desire to know her purpose. Amy had prayed to God asking him to let her know what her purpose in life was. After a few days it just came to her in thought. She was already living her purpose. Caregiving was her purpose in life. God had made it clear.

Besides caregiving in her family, she worked for eleven years with the disabled in a facility. After her mom died, Amy took over as caregiver and guardian for the sister she had helped since she was in kindergarten.

That's how it went throughout Amy's life. God kept bringing those who needed her care into her life, and there were several more. Amy stepped up to the challenge. She knew it was her life purpose. She was very good at it, caring with compassion and helping with the physical, but also caring for the entire well-being of those she loved and cared for. She addressed the complete package. Amy cared for their souls, too. She helped them look at what is most important… those things that meant the difference in where they would spend eternity. Just think of what heaven's job description for a position like Amy's looks like.

For we are God's handiwork,
created in Christ Jesus to do good works,
which God prepared in advance for us to do.

Ephesians 2:10 NIV

Pause to Ponder

Imagine, at five years old, being tasked to take care of your older sister and teach her all that you knew. Imagine the faith of a kindergartener who learned to talk to God all day long for any help that she needed in caring for her older sister. A faith that would lead to a life of caregiving for numerous people in many ways. Our life's purpose is our mission from above. Amy asked God to reveal her purpose. God answered her and revealed her purpose. Amy never turned down a job that God sent to her, despite the fact that many of those jobs were decades long.

Whenever you run into something that you need help with, talk to God. Pray. Depend on him.

Have you discovered your purpose? Are you fulfilling it? You can do this! Just follow the lead of a five-year-old. A five-year-old, responding to a nudge from God.

Pause for Prayer

Dear Lord,

Sometimes, we struggle with knowing our purpose. We know that you have a plan for each of us. Please help us discover our purpose in life. Confirm your plan for us. Give us the strength and the tools to fulfill that purpose. Encourage us when we are discouraged. Reassure us with your gentle calls. Thank you for having a plan for us. Nudge us when we aren't sure what we should be doing. We ask that you would give us satisfaction in fulfilling our life's purpose. Thank you, Lord. Thank you for sending us a Savior with the most important purpose in life. Thank you for his great sacrifice on our behalf. As we work to follow your plan for us, help us to see Jesus in our work. Please keep us on track and focused on you throughout our life.

We ask these things in Jesus's name.
Amen.

CHAPTER 26

Unfinished Business

Margaret didn't fear death any more than anyone else. She mostly feared the process of dying. It had been that way her entire life. That was about to change.

Margaret had a strong faith. She was in church every week. She had an active prayer life. She shared her faith with others. She relied on the Lord to get her through all the tough things in life.

Margaret was a hardworking woman, both on the job and at home. She was very strong on family ties. She kept a beautiful house and was a wonderful hostess. She loved her family and had a big heart for her children and grandchildren. Having a nice home was important to her. A nice home provided a place of peace. A sanctuary from the troubles of the world.

It was the early morning hours of Monday, June 1st, 2015. Margaret had gone to bed as usual and easily fell asleep. Later in the night she had gotten up to go to the bathroom. From then on, she has no recollection of what happened in this realm for the next eight hours.

Her husband, Daniel, remembers waking up in the middle of the night to all the lights in the house being on. Thinking that was strange, he got up. He could tell something was wrong with Margaret. She seemed disoriented and wasn't acting at all like herself. She kept asking Daniel if she had to go to work. She thought it was time to get ready for work, but Daniel told her it was the middle of the night. Daniel noticed some things that made him feel like she might be having a stroke. He told her they were going to the hospital. He told her to get dressed, although Margaret does not remember any of this.

While in the hospital, Margaret underwent many medical tests. Although the medical staff indicated that she did not have a stroke, they did confirm that she had a TIA (Transient Ischemic Attack). Some people call this a mini-stroke. Her husband called their children to fill them in, and they came to the hospital.

Although Margaret does not remember anything physical of her mini-stroke, she does remember an experience she had during that time. Suddenly, Margaret was floating. She was experiencing something she never had before. It was a very peaceful and tranquil time. She felt like she didn't have a care in the world.

Although both of her parents were deceased, she appeared to be in her parent's house. Her mom and dad were sitting by the kitchen table, talking to each other. She does not know what they were talking about. She wanted them to look up at her, but they did not. She remembers feeling sad that they didn't look up at her. She wanted to get their attention, but they seemed unaware of her presence.

Margaret liked where she was. This wonderful floating feeling made her feel like she was lightweight. She did not see herself, only her surroundings. Seeing her deceased mom and dad was amazing to her. This made her start thinking about her siblings that had passed on before her. No doubt, there were thoughts of heaven and eternal life.

Margaret knew she was someplace wonderful. She wanted to stay, but she felt a bit of conflict about that. She almost felt guilty about wanting to stay because in that moment, she wasn't concerned about her husband and children. She was feeling very content.

As her excitement for this new place increased, Margaret was told that it wasn't her time yet to pass into eternity. She very much wanted to be with her parents and siblings, who had gone on before her. She wanted to stay in this peaceful place, yet in her mind, she knew it just wasn't her time yet. And then suddenly, she was back. Back in this world. Back in her body. Margaret awoke to being rolled into a hospital room, where her family was waiting for her. She had lost eight hours of time that she remembers nothing about in this world. Those hours were from 1:30 AM until 10 AM.

She left that peaceful place with an acute awareness. A message was conveyed to her that she needed to be here on earth for a while yet. She strongly felt in her heart that she was needed here to take care of and love her family. It was a powerful awareness. She can see this and feel it with her husband and children.

What was Margaret's response to this incident and the message she received from it? She has said many prayers thanking God for bringing her back from the hours she doesn't recall. In time, she was able to return to work. It was difficult for Margaret to talk to her family about what she had experienced. She struggled with guilt over wanting to stay in that peaceful place. That peaceful place that was apart from her earthly family. She knew that peace was from God.

Margaret knew that God had some lessons for her. She feels that he wants her to see all the good things she had in her life before this incident and to appreciate and enjoy them the most. She knows that God has more love for her to give and more work for her to do here with her family. She knows these things because he put them in her heart. God nudged her. She has no doubt about that.

Margaret has no fear of death. She knows that there's something wonderful for believers to look forward to. As a believer, she knows she came back to finish up her work here on Earth. Her work here is to take care of and love her family. She has no doubt about it.

Until that time when she is free to go—that time when God calls her home, back to that peaceful place, she intends to carry out that work. And then it will come. Peace. That sweet peace that only God can give. Peace that will last forever in her heavenly home.

***

And we know that in all things
God works for the good of those who love him,
who have been called according to his purpose.

Romans 8:28 NIV

***

Pause to Ponder

Sometimes, we long to go home to heaven. Life on this earth has challenges and heartaches mixed in with love and wonderful times spent with our loved ones. Our bodies can experience issues and make life more challenging. Knowing that there is a better, more peaceful place to be could cause people to feel like they are being held back or denied. Margaret knows that God has her place ready in heaven. She knows that the words of John 14:2-3 are true. One day, when her work here is done, Jesus will take her home. Until that day, she cherishes her special assignment on earth caring for and loving her family.

❧

My Father's house has many rooms;
if that were not so,
would I have told you that I am going there
to prepare a place for you?
And if I go and prepare a place for you,
I will come back and take you to be with me
that you also may be where I am.

John 14:2-3 NIV

❧

Pause for Prayer

Dear Heavenly Father,

Thank you for your tender care. Thank you for life itself. Thank you for the work you have prepared for us to do on this earth. Help us to fulfill your purpose in that work. We pray that our work may be acceptable to you. When our work here is done and our appointed time has come, please take us to our heavenly home to be with you.

In Jesus's name.
Amen.

CHAPTER 27

Strength from Heaven

Life gets busy and as long as we are feeling good, we take much for granted. When the body starts to act out, life can quickly change. Hope had been having pain. She needed a hip replacement. It was not fun, but necessary to regain some quality of life. Hope took time off work to take care of the situation. She had the hip replaced, followed by two months of being in bed and lots of sleeping. It took a period of time, but she finally got life somewhat back to normal.

Time went by and Hope had more pain. She needed to get the second hip replacement done. Suddenly, a wave of family stress and turmoil began. Her niece had multiple health issues and was completely dependent on her full-time caregiver, Hope's sister. Unfortunately, her niece was scheduled for multiple major surgeries at this time. Her seventy-nine-year-old mom was experiencing congestive heart failure. It was recommended that her mom be put on hospice care. The family wanted to keep her at home and help care for her. The timing couldn't have been worse for Hope's surgery.

Being the oldest, Hope felt a need to be there for both her aging parents, as well as her sister and niece. The family knew Hope's mother was terminal with the hospice care, yet nobody knew how long her mom had. The timing of these things was in God's hands, and the family knew that. With the impending death of a parent comes much stress and many unknowns. The siblings on the scene get asked hard questions. "When should we come home?" some would ask. Other siblings were in denial. It seems during times of the impending death of a loved one, there are many emotional and relationship issues that hang over people. There's sometimes unfinished business the loved one has to deal with, and at times, they need help from their family to accomplish that. They may need to heal some old wounds or mend a relationship.

There is much to think about. You want to be there for them. With two siblings in denial about what was happening and one sibling completely immersed in caregiving for a child who was scheduled for several major surgeries, it seemed Hope, the oldest sibling, was going to need to be available and step up to help her mom find the closure she needed to prepare for leaving this world.

Hope's mom had experienced a near-death situation. She had been told it was not her time yet. "You have two more things to do," she was told. The family struggled to gain insight into that message. They thought they knew one of the two things. Their mom accomplished the first thing. They really weren't sure about the second thing.

It was a stressful time. There were doctor visits and coordination with doctors and nurses. Hope wasn't sure how she was going to be there for her family and deal with the impact of the hip surgery. She knew there was only one way she could cope with all of this. She prayed. She asked God to help her deal with it all. She needed his help with her physical pain and limitations, emotional support, and the ability to help her family. She put her faith in God's ways and boldly stepped forward.

Meanwhile, Hope needed her hip replacement, and her niece needed to have multiple surgeries. There was no waiting. It all had to be done.

As Hope's mom struggled with congestive heart failure, her niece had her surgeries. With her niece's surgeries completed, there were many medical concerns still hanging over her. Once again, in faith, Hope moved forward, trusting that God had her back. She had her second hip replacement the day following her niece's surgery.

God answered Hope's prayer request to allow her to be able to help her parents following her surgery. Hope very quickly was at her mom's side and helped her folks in any way that she could. Hope's parents needed help with legal paperwork. There were preparations to make to get affairs in order. It was all overwhelming and even more distressing because of the condition of Hope's mom. Hope's folks couldn't believe how well Hope was doing after her hip replacement surgery. She was up and walking around. She shouldn't have been able to do that yet. She was able to help her mom and dad and be there for her sister and niece. It was an amazing time to see God's hand in carrying her through these storms in life allowing her to do what she needed to do without pain and suffering so quickly after surgery.

Hope's mom knew that her time was coming soon. She had no doubt. In fact, one day, she announced she was going to die the next day. The next day came, and she passed away, just as she had said.

Hope was able to be there for her mom until the end. She was able to help plan the arrangements, all so very soon after having the hip replacement. She was able to walk about and do things. She was even doing these things without her walker and without pain. Her body had virtually had no downtime for rest and recovery because of all the family trials that had been going on and the demands that were placed on Hope. Everyone was amazed that this could be!

The following week after her mom died, Hope was back to using her walker. Her body was reverting to a recuperation stage. It now needed healing time and rest. Even three and a half months post-surgery, Hope was still recuperating, yet right after surgery, she was fully functional. In an amazing way, God had given her a temporary reprieve from the healing journey. He answered her prayers so that she could be available to help her mom, sister, and niece through a difficult time. When that was over, he let her body resume where he had intervened so that it could have time to heal. What an amazing God we have!

✺

The LORD is near to all who call on him,
to all who call on him in truth.
He fulfills the desires of those who fear him;
he hears their cry and saves them.

Psalm 145:18-19 NIV

✺

Pause to Ponder

Isn't it strange how life can suddenly throw so many hurdles at you simultaneously? Isn't it overwhelming when that happens? When you are a child, where do you go first when troubles come your way? You go to your mother or father. You know they will help you through it. You trust them. As adults, some of us forget that. At times, we just want to throw our hands in the air and give up or crawl into a fetal position and ask someone to wake us up when it's all over. The first place Hope turned was to her Heavenly Father. She knew she could not handle this alone. She knew he had the solutions she could not come up with on her own. So she asked for them. She trusted God for the solution. For the help and the strength that she needed. Hope was not disappointed.

Pause for Prayer

Dear Heavenly Father,

Life can be hard. Emotionally. Physically. Yes, even spiritually. There are times we feel at a complete loss of what to do. The challenges are too many. The pain is too real. Help us to remember that we have someone to go to. Remind us to come to you in prayer first. Strengthen us. Help us in our decision-making. Heal us. Comfort us. Help us to care for ourselves and others as you care for us.

In Jesus's name.
Amen.

CHAPTER 28

Twisted Thinking

It was a beautiful fall day. The sun was shining. The temperature was working its way up towards 86 degrees. There were many errands to run, but she knew she just had to take her time and savor one of these beautiful remaining fall days. Sara had to stop at the jewelry store that day. As she was about to park the car, she decided to pull ahead…all the way up to the end of the block.

Putting the car in park, Sara noticed two women standing in front of the building on the corner. They were holding pre-printed signs. She had always wondered about this building. Now, these women had her attention. The building had long stood there looking rather plain with simple signage. It had a non-committal name. "Options" was the name on the sign. That had always concerned Sara. It gave the appearance of being a medical clinic. Just the same, she had always wondered if it might be an abortion clinic. It was located in an older part of town and the way it appeared, it just seemed a little different. It seemed it would have been a good location for such a place.

As she got out of the car, Sara took a quick look at the women's signs. They referenced abortion as taking lives. Yes, they were pro-life, it was clear. Sara felt drawn to them. "Hello," she said as she approached them. Sara could tell they weren't sure how to respond. "Is this an abortion clinic?" she asked them. "They say they aren't," one of the women said, "but we know that in the least, they give referrals for abortions," she said. She went on to say that there had been some recent changes and that they now had gone under the umbrella of a national organization that was very supportive of and a provider of abortions. Sara noticed the change in the signage on the building as the woman was telling this.

As Sara looked at her, she caught a glimpse of a necklace she was wearing. Clearly, it was a Christian symbol. "Thank you for what you are doing," Sara said to her. She asked them if they worked with a specific pro-life group. They named one that Sara had never heard of before. As they had a brief chat, the women told Sara they weren't used to being thanked for the work they do. One of the women said that most people did not support them in their efforts. Hearing that made Sara feel very sad.

The three of them spoke briefly about how much society has changed in the past few years. One of the women stated that fifty years ago, they never would have imagined that things would have reached such a state by now. They knew abortions happened back then, but they all agreed that one never would have thought things would have reached the point that selling aborted baby parts would be a lucrative business.

Sara told them of her past involvement in efforts to save the unborn. She told them of the unspeakable pictures she had been shown of aborted babies all those years ago...babies that had been literally torn apart by the abortion procedure. They spoke to Sara of the horrors of full-term babies in this day and age being born alive after a botched abortion and then killed by doctors. They were having a hard time grasping how anyone could disagree with the fact that this was murder.

By now, their little gathering was apparently getting some attention. Sara had wondered if the workers inside would be getting nervous about her standing outside talking to these ladies holding the signs. Suddenly, a young man, who appeared to be about twenty, came running across the street towards them. He, too, was holding a sign. As he came to a stop, he stood with his back towards the street and faced the other two women. "How peculiar," Sara thought. She couldn't read his entire sign, but the biggest and boldest word on the sign was "Love". He didn't say a word. He just stood there…with his back still towards the street.

The longer this uncomfortable situation continued, the more curious Sara was about the sign he was holding. As she strained to see more of it, she could tell there was a list of all the people we should love. It listed Blacks, Whites, Asians, Hispanics, and so on. Sara smiled. She thought, "Yes, we should love all those." Yet, there was still something strange going on here. Sara strained and craned some more to see the rest of the list on his love sign. It went on to list lesbians, gays, bisexuals, transsexuals. "Yes", she thought again. "We should love all people. We may not agree with their lifestyle and their life choices, but we should still love them." This sign and the young man's posture still seemed strange to her. How was this related to the abortion situation? And why was he standing with his back to the street?

As the two women and Sara continued their conversation, one of the women said something about abortion taking the life of a baby. Now, the young man couldn't help himself. He just had to say something.

"It's not taking a life," he said. "It's part of the woman. It's her choice to do what she wants because it is part of her."

The two women and Sara were speechless at this point. Obviously, they did not want this to become confrontational, but they were at a loss of what to say. One of the women tried to explain to him that abortion really is taking a life. Sara went on to say that anyone who has ever witnessed photos as she had of an aborted baby would have no doubt that a life had been taken. The women agreed and said that society doesn't want those kinds of photos shown anymore. They agreed that society is being manipulated and brainwashed to sugarcoat what reality is in this day and age. Sara also told the young man that one day, there would be accountability for all the abortions that had ever happened. She was not sure if he knew what she was referring to or not.

After visiting a bit, Sara excused herself and went to the jewelry store. On returning to her car, the young man was still standing there holding his love sign. The two women smiled and waved at Sara as she got in the car and pulled away.

Sara had several errands to run and put the whole thing out of her mind until she got home and was done with the day's work. It was then, after having time to reflect, that it occurred to her. There were two opportunities presented to her that afternoon. One was the chance to encourage fellow Christians in their work, which she had done. The other was the chance to witness to someone who clearly had twisted thinking about the sanctity of life.

Although Sara had participated in some discussions with the young man, she could have done better. Why is it that when we most need to witness to someone we are most at a loss of words? Why is it that sometimes after an opportunity presents itself we finally think of something appropriate, meaningful, even clever and effective, that we could have said? It seems frustrating, but so often the case.

As the evening went on, thoughts of the young man with the twisted thinking kept coming to mind. Sara kept thinking of his love sign. She thought of all kinds of things that she could have and should have said. But now the opportunity was lost.

"I really like your love sign," Sara could have said. "I agree with you, we should love everyone, even if we don't agree with their lifestyle or their life choices. But I have a question for you. I am a bit confused about your sign. I am confused about the irony of your sign. How does taking a life relate to love? If a woman is supposed to love, what is loving about taking a life—the life that is within her?" And then, when the young man counter-acted with, "But it's not a life…it is part of a woman," Sara could have responded with "If it is part of a woman, then why does it have its own heart?" She could have quoted Psalm 139:13 NIV.

For you created my inmost being;
you knit me together in my mother's womb.

Psalm 139:13 NIV

She could have said, "Does that not sound like a separate life within the mother? And does ripping that life out of the woman and snuffing it out sound like love to you? It surely doesn't to me." Or…she could have said, "I really like your love sign, but you forgot one group of people on it." When he asked who he left out, she could have simply said, "Unborn babies. We need to love unborn babies." She could have gone on to remind him that he and Sara were once unborn babies, too. They were the same as they are now, only smaller.

And then she could have added more. There is Ecclesiastes 11:5 NLT.

❧

"Just as you cannot understand the path of the wind
or the mystery of a tiny baby growing in its mother's womb,
so you cannot understand the activity of God,
who does all things."

Ecclesiastes 11:5 NLT

❧

The Bible calls the unborn "a tiny baby growing in its mother's womb." The Bible clearly recognizes that baby as not part of the mother, but rather a separate being, a baby, a body growing inside of the mother.

Sara could have added more, but…she hadn't. She hadn't thought of it at the right time. She hadn't said it. She had missed an opportunity. God nudged her to remember that she needs to be ready to witness at any time to any person. Sara vaguely remembered there was a Bible verse about this very topic. He nudged her to remember that in this day and age, we are seeing a lot of twisted thinking. People are getting numb to what is right and wrong. Their reasoning is not always reasonable. The news media, social media, some schools, many politicians, and the sinful world are all compounding this problem. And the more exposure people get to this twisted thinking, the more they buy into it. Eventually, they can't think for themselves but rather accept what they are spoon-fed by the twisted thinkers, especially if it appeals to them.

God nudged Sara to remember that she needed to arm herself with his Word. He nudged her to remember to call out to him in prayer and ask him to send the Holy Spirit to give her the right words at the right time to serve his purpose. Sara may not know what to say to a given person at a given time, but the Holy Spirit will know. He will lead Sara, and he will lead you if you call on him.

Through this encounter, God nudged Sara to remember that we have to be on guard. We need to bring our A game when it comes to saving souls. We have to be ready to make that free throw at a moment's notice. It could end up being the difference between winning and losing. In some instances, it could be the difference between life and death.

***

… Always be prepared to give an answer
to everyone who asks you to give the reason
for the hope that you have.
But do this with gentleness and respect,
keeping a clear conscience,
so that those who speak maliciously
against your good behavior in Christ
may be ashamed of their slander.

1 Peter 3:15-16 NIV

***

Pause to Ponder

We are living in an age of twisted thinking. Sometimes, the things we hear are alarming.

What is right is presented to us as wrong. What is wrong is presented to us as right. Morals and ethics have all but disappeared. We are told things that we know to be immoral are the correct way to live. Truth is almost a collector item. Sometimes, truth is even unrecognizable.

How do we stay grounded while surrounded by so much twisted thinking? And, how do we help others see they are being influenced by twisted thinking?

We are on call to counteract twisted thinking. We need to be in prayer. We need to arm ourselves with God's Word. We need to call on the Holy Spirit to give us the right words at the right time, even if it means a delay in running our endless list of errands.

Pause for Prayer

Dear Heavenly Father,

Our hearts grieve at the condition of society. We struggle with the loss of respect for the sanctity of life. We mourn the loss of more than 63 million babies since 1973 through this barbaric act of abortion. We ask you to send your Holy Spirit to minister to the hearts of those with twisted thinking. We pray that you would nudge them, yes, move their hearts to grasp the truth that life begins at conception. Lead them to stop supporting abortion. Help those who have had abortions to repent and accept your forgiveness. Lead them to a life of clearer thinking. Lead them to live their lives for you. Help our lawmakers and judges to stop playing God and value life as your creation. Give us the right words to say to others on this topic at just the right time. Give us the courage to speak out.

We ask these things in Jesus's precious name.
Amen.

CHAPTER 29

Sunday Morning Circus

Oh, the frustration! Oh, the stress! You get that harried feeling. The kids are dragging their feet. One is still eating. One is waiting for you to get the snarls out of her hair. Where is your Sunday School Teacher's Guide? Who messed with the activity crafts you were working on last night? Your husband is antsy to leave. You look in the mirror. Oh my! You forgot to clean the smudges off your eyelids from putting on mascara. Does Katie have a pen and paper for her sermon notes? As you finally get everyone out the door, you think of it. Did you put the meatloaf in the oven and turn on the oven timer? As you walk into church, you collapse in the pew. But the morning circus is not over. It has just moved the spotlight to shine on other challenges.

During the Sunday morning circus, there's not one, not two, but a three-ring show going on…in church, of all places! And in Ring 1, a harried-looking Mom faces off with Tantrum Toddler. In Ring 2, see Dad giving "the look" to his primary grade son, who is pulling on his sister's ponytail. Ring 3, well, that's where the clowns are performing…free giggles for all.

Jesus loved children. We love children. They can be so innocent and sweet. They can also be a handful when in church! Anyone raising children can recall more than one wild and crazy Sunday morning as the family scurried to get ready for church and get there on time. Settling into the pew and thinking the most challenging part was behind them, many parents soon learned the antics were only starting. Was it difficult? Yes. Was it sometimes downright crazy? Yes!

Parents with babies have extra preparation, distractions, and struggles in church. There are bulging diaper bags to contend with, interrupting nap times for babies, and in the winter, juggling with snowsuits.

There's quite an assortment of little personalities sitting in the pews. There is the pew-kicker, the flirt, the crier, the toy-thrower, the head-banger, the hymnal-defacer, the talker, the leaner, the tease, the sneaky sibling, the can't sit-stiller, the head-turner, the run-away, the sleeper, and the cuddler.

What does Rachel remember? The first cry room their church had. A friend, Laura, lobbying for a nursing room for moms with infants. Sitting in a church filled with teens, young children, and babies...many babies! She remembers large Sunday school classes and the back pews in her church filled with young families.

Was she ever tempted to give up and stay home? Occasionally, but mostly not. It was important to her that her kids had God in their life. It was important to her that they grew up with a habit of going to church on Sunday.

Children can grasp onto faith in an accepting way that we as adults should observe. Children are truly a blessing and can bring us some good giggles from God. They can also grasp some Christian concepts and teach us along the way. They have a way of expressing things in such a simplistic way, that it can impact us as adults. Surely that is a God-thing...that our children can teach us a thing or two!

Now, Rachel's children are grown and married. She has grandchildren that are growing up quickly. And what is it that she remembers about her children and grandchildren in church? She remembers some special things. She likes to call them "Giggles from God".

Rachel remembers chubby fingers grasping hymn books years before the child could read. She remembers sweet voices attempting to sing praises to God with the congregation before they could speak words. She remembers folded hands and bowed heads with one eye open to see what was going on. She remembers hearing the clanking of a quarter her little one put in the offering plate as it went by. She remembers her kids proudly showing her their Sunday school papers after class as they waited for church to start. She loved hearing their version of the Bible stories they learned that day. She remembers holding her children on her lap and loving that they were all sitting there together in the Lord's house.

Rachel has many memories of those days. Little bags of dry cereal appeared from purses while dainty fingers picked pieces out one by one and put them in their mouth. Picture books were examined and dropped under and behind pews. Irresistible grins and baby flirts caused even the most serious churchgoers to temporarily lose their focus. Parents hiked toddlers on their hips as they went to the altar for communion. The pastor smiled and blessed them as he went down the railing while giving the Lord's Supper.

With all the memories of those days, Rachel doesn't remember much of the difficult times. Just when she would wonder if it was worth it…just when she would wonder if any of them would get anything out of the service…just when she was ready to tell herself maybe they should wait until the kids were older, God gave her some comic relief. Even though it was a challenge at the time, Rachel doesn't remember much of the stress because it was all worth it. She would never have denied her children those opportunities to be in the Lord's house, even though it was some very wild days when it was happening. It was worth every bit of it!

What Rachel's children learned in church spilled over into everyday life. In the 1970s, when Katie was about four years old, Rachel and John took a family trip to see the Arch in St Louis. As John and Rachel walked around the spacious grounds there, they saw some young people meandering through the grounds. Suddenly, Katie got very excited. She pointed to someone and said loudly, "Jesoo!" She couldn't say Jesus. It was always Jesoo. John and Rachel looked. Before them stood a young man with long brown hair flowing to his shoulders. He was wearing loose clothing. He did bear some resemblance to the pictures of Jesus depicted in the children's Bible story books. Katie was excited to see who she thought was Jesus--the one who loves her--the one she had been learning about in church and Sunday school and from her Bible stories at home.

When Rachel's children were young, she also taught Sunday school. One year when she had the kindergarten class, she was covering a lesson about giving. Holding up a picture of a large and flat brass offering plate, Rachel asked the 5-year-olds if they knew what that was. One of them said, "Yeah, that's a dog dish!"

Katie loved to sing hymns. At about six years old, she sat down at a friend's piano and started playing hymns she had learned to sing in her Christian elementary school. She played those songs by ear. She did not have access to a piano at home. She hadn't had a lesson! Katie loved sitting on Rachel's lap while she read Bible stories to her. Katie loved saying grace before meals and bedtime prayers.

Eventually, Katie's brother came along. Noah was one of the church-eaters. Regardless of the breakfast situation that day, he invariably expected his treat while sitting in the pew. One Sunday, the treat wasn't forthcoming soon enough. Suddenly, at a quiet point in the service, Noah shouted, "I want my waisins!" Adult shoulders bounced up and down as people tried to contain their laughter. His grandmother heard him several pews ahead.

Years later, Noah's son, Ethan, would make his own announcement in church. After the choir finished a beautiful song and the church grew silent, Ethan announced with a loud voice, "Allllllll done!"

Not long after that, Rachel and John traveled to spend Easter with Tiffany, Noah, and the grandchildren. Rachel had bought the grandkids each a dressy new outfit to wear for Easter. A pretty pink ruffly dress for Kylee. A Navy blue dress pants and a matching vest for Ethan with a light blue dress shirt and matching tie. Ethan was about three years old. Later that afternoon, the kids were still dressed up. After a nice Easter dinner, everyone went outside to bask in the warm sunshine and watch the kids hunt for Easter Eggs. Ethan bent over to pick up an egg. It appeared his new pants had a weird pucker in the back. Ethan's mom, Tiffany, had not dressed him that morning as she had left early so that she could teach Sunday school. Tiffany said, "Who dressed Ethan this morning?" Noah said that he had. Tiffany pointed out that Ethan's pants were on backward, which meant they were on backward in church. Ethan had spent considerable time standing on the pew seat, which means the people behind him were well aware of the status of his backward pants!

Ethan's sister, Kylee, was a beautiful baby with big blue eyes. She always attracted a lot of attention because of it. With a doting mom and three doting grandmas, there were always plenty of photo sessions from early on. As Kylee got to be a toddler and preschooler, she would stop, pose, and flash her best smile as soon as she saw someone holding a camera. One day in church, someone was passing by and made a comment about what a pretty child Kylee was. Kylee was looking the other way, but as soon as she heard the comment, she went into her model mode. She quickly turned her head, posed, and put on her best smile. She must have been sorely disappointed when she saw there was no camera awaiting her.

It appears to be universal in every church. Brothers and sisters squirm. They pick at each other. They need to be separated by Mom and Dad. They write on church bulletins and sometimes in hymnals. They get away from their parents and crawl under pews. They pull people's hair and make cooing sounds. They sometimes cry. They hit their head. Of course, not on the soft velvety cushion, but on the hard oak edging of the pews. This is followed by a few seconds of unexpected silence as they hold their breath. Then we wait...there it is... intense cries and a waterfall of tears. Babies choke their Moms with her own necklace. Toddlers hang over the back of the pew. They smile, they wave, and they say, "Bah, Bye!" They want to give you something. They throw their pacifier on the floor. They throw their book on the floor and smile as they wait for you to pick it up, not once, not twice, but over and over. If you make eye contact with them...well, it's all over; they won't quit! And you know you love it!

Does any of that bother Rachel? No. She loves seeing parents bring their children to God's house. Rachel loves the reminders of when her children were little.

So let them eat their waisins. Let them search the crowd for Jesoo. Let them put their quarters in the dog dish. They are learning. As you collapse onto the pew on those hectic Sunday mornings, you may be blessed with some stress-relieving giggles from God. You may be blessed with a nudge from God. And you will know. You will know that the Sunday morning circus really is worth it.

Hopefully, some years later, that grown child will sit on a pew as a parent and deal with their children during their own Sunday morning circus. Although she loves the giggles, Rachel knows it's about sitting in the pew. It's about starting the habit. It's about doing what God nudged you to do.

Rachel knows it really is about the destiny of little souls. Little souls on their way to becoming adults. Adults that we want to see in heaven someday.

❦

Start children off on the way they should go,
and even when they are old they will not turn from it.

Proverbs 22:6 NIV

❦

Pause to Ponder

Seeing those little ones come to church reminds Rachel that her church is alive and teeming with a new generation coming to the Lord. That is something every congregation wants to have happen. So let them come. Let them come to Jesus. The kingdom of heaven belongs to them. Jesus said so.

When they come, we will welcome them. When they come, we will keep our focus on the sermon. When they come, we may have a moment where we can't help but smile. We may even get a giggle from God.

Just when taking the little ones to church seems to be so challenging, so overwhelming, so exhausting, God gives a gentle nudge. He gives us a chuckle to relieve the stress. He floods our hearts with feelings of love and appreciation for our children and grandchildren. Those little high-pitched voices say something that reminds us why we are doing what we do. God nudges us with a Bible verse that tells us this is where he wants them to be. He nudges us with reminders that he expects us to do this.

Is it worth it? Why are you doing it, anyway? What is the benefit? Do they even know what is going on?

You are creating a habit. You are bringing them to the Lord's house. Why? Because he wants you to. He said so in the Bible. Let the little children come unto me. Train up a child in the way he should go. God is nudging you. Are you listening? Are you responding? Will it be worth it? Absolutely! You are investing in your child's future. It is one of your biggest responsibilities as a parent.

Eventually, that child will know the difference between the offering plate and a dog dish. Eventually, that child will learn that church isn't where we go to eat our raisins. And yes, that child will even learn that we don't have to go to the Arch in St Louis to find Jesus. In time, that child will learn that there is no better place to be on Sunday morning, even if their pants are on backward.

Pause for Prayer

Dear Lord,

We ask that you send your Holy Spirit to touch hearts, to move them, to nudge them to return to you and your house of worship. We ask that you bring back the children to your house of worship.

We thank you for godly parents who faithfully bring little souls to your house of worship. We ask that you send your Holy Spirit to encourage and strengthen them. Keep them steadfast in raising their children in accordance with your will.

We ask that you also send your Holy Spirit to the children. Please minister to them and grow their faith as they are growing up in such a challenging world. Teach them of your love and forgiveness. Expose them to your true Word. Let them hunger for this Word.

Be with the Christian day school teachers and Sunday school teachers as they help guide the children in living their lives for you. Be with the pastors as they teach God's Word to them. May we, as a congregation, support the children as they learn about you. Help us to reach out to others who are unchurched. Help parents and grandparents to be an example to the children of the life you want them to lead.

Thank you for the blessing of these children, Lord. We take comfort in knowing that you hold them in the palm of your hand. We know that you want the little children to come to you. We also know that even a child can bring others to Christ. Help us to do right by these little ones. We entrust these precious children to your care.

In Jesus's name.
Amen.

CHAPTER 30

A Heart for the Homeless

She had a big heart and a big personality. She enjoyed life and lived it to the fullest. Her interests were varied. She loved to go camping, to travel, and visit family and friends. She loved dancing. Despite all this, she knew she had a calling. "Just one person can make a difference," she would say. God had filled her heart with tenderness towards the homeless.

It all started when Rita started doing a soup kitchen after a move. She felt sorry for those who did not have their basic needs met. She ached for those who had no gloves or hat in the cold weather. She shuddered when she saw the homeless in the rain without an umbrella. She felt compassion for all those living without any shelter.

Rita has worked at homeless shelters for forty years through her church. This work increased her awareness of those who did not go to shelters or have access to them.

When Rita looks at the homeless she sees someone who needs a helping hand. She sees someone without protection from the elements. Someone who is enduring the cold, the heat, the rain, the blizzards, the wind, and the storms. As she looks at them she thinks of what they are thinking. They wish that they had made better choices in life, and yet, haven't we all made some poor decisions in life? They wish that others would see them as people and not ignore them.

God had also instilled in Rita a longing to help the homeless. Those members of society that many look away from were magnetic to her. Those dirty people that lived by the tracks, under the bridge, in the park. Those people wearing ragged clothes and holey shoes. You know, the ones with everything they own in a grocery cart. Yeah, the cart was probably stolen for all we know. Yes, those same people who walk the streets much of the day and hang out at the laundromat at night. Yep, and that shivering old woman you saw dumpster diving behind the store last week. And yes, that old man that wears the black wool suit when it is 90 degrees outside. Don't forget the tall man with the noticeable limp that walks up and down the same street all day long every day.

Rita looked at those people and saw Jesus in their eyes. The words of Matthew 25 compelled her to act.

❦

"The King will reply,
'Truly I tell you, whatever you did for one of the least of
these brothers and sisters of mine, you did for me.'
"Then he will say to those on his left,
'Depart from me, you who are cursed,
into the eternal fire prepared for the devil and his angels.
For I was hungry and you gave me nothing to eat,
I was thirsty and you gave me nothing to drink,
I was a stranger and you did not invite me in,
I needed clothes and you did not clothe me,
I was sick and in prison and you did not look after me.'

"They also will answer,
'Lord, when did we see you hungry or thirsty
or a stranger or needing clothes or sick or in prison,
and did not help you?'
"He will reply, 'Truly I tell you,
whatever you did not do for one of the least of these,
you did not do for me.'

Matthew 25:40-45 NIV

With a heart full of compassion, Rita knew she had to do something to help. While many looked down on the homeless in disgust, Rita looked at those same people and saw their needs. She saw humanity going without basic necessities. She knew even though she was just one person, she could make a difference to one or more of them. God touched her heart. He nudged her. When God nudges you, you just can't ignore it. She knew she needed to act.

Rita regularly takes little homemade personal care kits with her when she has outings so she is prepared when she has an encounter with the homeless. Inside the care kits, she puts socks, water, snacks, hand sanitizers, and two large garbage sacks to use as a raincoat or to cover the ground to lie down on. She never gives them money. One never knows what will happen with these homeless encounters. Many of them wouldn't be a problem, but some might be dealing with substance abuse or mental health issues. It could get dangerous. You just don't know what will happen. There is definitely some risk involved. Rita had her system in place to make her deliveries as safe as possible. When you are on a mission from God, you've also got some special protection, as well. Rita's experiences with the homeless are varied.

One day, Rita was headed to Walmart. A gentleman who appeared to be homeless was sitting on the curb of the parking lot. He was not actively begging. Nudged! Rita turned back and asked if he wanted a goody bag. He stood up and said, "Yes." After accepting the bag, he turned and said, "Thank you, Jesus." Rita deduced that he must have been praying for some help.

Another time, Rita and her husband, Jacob, were driving in Chicago. They saw a man walking on the median between several lanes of traffic. Rita asked Jacob to slow down. She called out to the man. After she called out, he looked so dejected and sad. She thought he was preparing himself to be called names or made fun of. She asked the man if he wanted a goody bag. She always asks. As she handed him the bag, he said, "Thank you." Looking at him, she saw the eyes of Jesus. It might only be a bottle of water, but it can make a difference.

In time, Rita started packing goody bags in a big suitcase. She would take the train to downtown Chicago to hand them out. One day, a lady walked up to her and very aggressively said, "Give me something for food." Rita felt that the woman was tired of being ignored. Rita gave her a goody bag and kept walking. The woman looked through the bag, turned towards Rita, and said, "Thank you for doing that." Rita said, "You're welcome." The woman's demeanor had completely changed. Rita had made a difference for her.

Another time, Rita had gotten off the train and walked up the street while handing out three goody bags. When she asks people if they want a goody bag and they hesitate, she tells them what is in there. A man behind her noticed what she was doing. He came up to Rita and said, "That is very nice of you." Rita hopes that if anyone observes what she is doing that they will be inspired to do a kind act also. One never knows who is watching.

Once, Rita had her husband drop her off at a corner so she could hand out a bag. A man was resting on a bench. She asked if he wanted a bag. He said no. She said, "I have socks." "You do?"

he said. "Yes," said Rita, "and homemade cookies." "Cookies?" he asked. "Yes," said Rita, "and a shirt." The man went through the bag that was generously packed with many things. He took one-half of the items. As he and Rita talked, he asked her if she was with an organization or doing this on her own. People of some faiths try to help the homeless and then try to convert them. This has caused the homeless to be cautious.

Another day, Rita saw a man standing on a curb by a turn lane. The man was begging. Rita was going in the opposite direction, so she parked her car and walked back to hand him a bag. She then went on to the store she had been headed towards. A woman came up to her and asked if she was the person who handed the bag to the man. Thanking Rita, the woman went on to tell Rita that her brother had mental issues and was living on the streets. She told Rita that she also tried to help the homeless.

Everyone has their own story. We are all human beings. It is sad to see how often we forget about those less fortunate. Rita believes we can make a difference. She also thinks we can inspire others to do a kind act, too. It doesn't have to be a grand act. Something as easy as handing out water bottles or a soft snack bar can make all the difference to someone. You never know when you might be an answer to someone's prayers. Do you feel a nudge in your heart? Rita did, and she acted. She's been responding to God's nudges for forty years.

Rita is thankful that the Lord has kept her safe while handing out her goody bags. She gives thanks for friends who have gone with her in twenty degrees below zero temperatures to hand out food and hand warmers. She's thankful for her husband who drops her off and waits while keeping watch as she delivers goody bags.

Rita's nudges from God keep coming. And Rita keeps responding. One particular day was cold, windy, and wet. With the miserable weather conditions, Rita's heart was heavy for the homeless. You see, Rita was a "stalker". She stalked the homeless. The last three times she had been stalking the homeless she found none. Most people would be glad to not find any homeless, but not Rita. She knew there were unmet needs out there somewhere.

She had recently read a newspaper article about a mission downtown that put coats, gloves, and hats out on a fence for the homeless to take as needed. Self-service freebies for the homeless. Unfortunately, Rita had forgotten the article at home. The article had the address of the freebie homeless fence. She had gone out to run errands and to look for the homeless. Again, she saw no homeless. She decided to head home since she did not have the freebie homeless fence address with her. She was not familiar with the area she was in. Rita has no built-in compass. As she puts it, "I get lost going around the block…seriously!" Now, of all times, when she was already lost, her GPS was not working. Since she didn't know where to go, it looked like she would not be helping the homeless today. Feeling disappointed, Rita tried to find her way to a street she knew so she could find her way back home. Suddenly, she encountered the mission with the freebie homeless fence. She put her items on the fence and returned to her car. As she was leaving the parking lot, she looked back. One of the coats she had just put on the fence was already gone!

With a heart full of love, she did act. Rita made a difference. Having no address with her to find the fence, then getting lost, with no working GPS and no inward sense of direction, she likely would not have found the fence on her own. But God had a mission for her. And someone needed a coat on a cold and rainy day. Despite the odds being against the delivery of that coat to a homeless person, it happened. "This," said Rita, "is how God works!" And God brings to completion another successful nudge. That nudge, perhaps, but there will be more. Rita knows that because God has touched her heart to help the homeless. And very soon now, Rita will be back out there once again…stalking…for the homeless. Responding to the nudges. Because this is the way that God works.

❧

Whoever is kind to the poor lends to the Lord,
and he will reward them for what they have done.

Proverbs 19:17 NIV

❧

Pause to Ponder

It is easy for us to look down on the outcast. It is easy to judge and put all the homeless into a category—a category that we make up and give certain attributes to. Homeless people don't all fit into one category. Bad things can happen to any of us. No one growing up says, "I want to be homeless!" Given the right circumstances, any one of us could be living under such depressing and stressful circumstances.

Imagine not having a dry, safe, and comfortable place to lie down at night. Imagine not being able to take that warm shower every morning. Think about the gnawing feeling in your stomach when a meal is long overdue. Imagine that happening every day. Think of not having a toothbrush and toothpaste. Rita does. She sees all those dilemmas. She responds to those needs with a heart full of compassion. She responds to the nudge that God puts on her heart.

Pause for Prayer

Dear Father in heaven,

Thank you for all the everyday necessities that you give us that we sometimes take for granted. Thank you for caring people giving of themselves to help others with those same basic needs. Please lead us with that example so that we, too, help those unable to help themselves. Help us to respond to your nudges as you told us to do in the Bible. As we do so, keep us safe and filled with compassion for others.

In Jesus's name.
Amen.

CHAPTER 31

The Power of a Mother's Prayer

It was summertime. A time of fun activities and school vacation. Her twin boys were 18 years old. It was a time in life where mothers take joy in seeing their children becoming adults. It is also a time in life where parents can't help but worry.

Lucas had just gotten a sport bike. A crotch rocket is what they called it. It was a very high-powered motorcycle. The kind you see people hunched over leaning far forward as they drive at high speeds down the highway. It was loud and it was powerful. Yes, that's a scary thing for a mom.

Diana, like any Mom, had concerns for her son's safety. She had told Lucas to be home by 10:30 that night. He said, "Okay!" and off he went. Just as promised, he pulled into the driveway at 10:30. His mom breathed a sigh of relief. Lucas came in and told her he was home, only to leave again at 10:35!

Diana went to bed, but she couldn't sleep. She lay there tossing and turning. Worrying and fearful. All she could think about was her son driving that high-powered cycle. She just wanted him to be safe. She got on her knees and gave her worries to the Lord. "Lord, I trust you with my son. Even if he's lying dead in a ditch, I trust you will be with him." After she turned her concerns over to the Lord, she felt complete relief from worry. She went back to bed and fell asleep. It was a pleasant, sweet sleep. It was the kind of sleep referenced in Proverbs 3:24. Her fears were gone. She trusted God would care for Lucas if anything bad ever happened.

⁓

When you lie down, you will not be afraid;
when you lie down, your sleep will be sweet.

Proverbs 3:24 NIV

⁓

Diana had decided to trust God and not fear. She was letting her faith handle this. That was the reason she could sleep.

Over time, as a mother, she placed her confidence in the Lord regarding her sons. She continued praying that the Lord would keep them safe. That if anything should happen to them, that he not let them be alone.

One evening, one and a half years later, that faith and trust would be fully activated. There was a knock on the door. There stood the deputy sheriff. Diana knew this was probably not good news. The female deputy told Diana she was chasing her son in her car. Lucas had been going over 100 miles per hour. He had rolled the car over seven times. He was ejected 50 feet from the vehicle. When the deputy got to her son, he was lying lifeless in the field. He had no pulse, and he wasn't breathing. This was not good. The deputy straightened his airway. He took a gasp of air. They had to med flight him to a hospital.

As the deputy explained what had happened, Diana's knees buckled. She didn't expect her son to live. She immediately got a prayer team together to start praying for her son. She then went to the hospital and continued to pray for him there.

Three days later, her son woke up from his coma. He said, "Mom, I need to talk to that boy." There was a sense of urgency in his voice. She told him the deputy said he was alone in that field. Her son insisted that he needed to talk to that boy. He described the boy as having curly blonde hair and blue eyes. He was sure the boy was a real person. He told her that the boy had been with him the entire time he was lying in that field.

Diana knew this was a direct answer to her prayers. Amazingly, Lucas made a good recovery from his injuries. God came through for her during one of her most difficult times. He cared for her son when no one else could. He comforted her son when even a mother couldn't. And he did so in an amazing way. Diana knew, without a doubt, that God was answering her prayers. She felt blessed because God gave her and her son some very special attention that day. She cried out in faith and she prayed. God heard her cries and he answered.

It was a year and a half earlier that Diana had started praying to God about her son's safety. She asked that God would be with her son and watch over him, especially during times of danger, even if he were lying dead in a ditch. She didn't want her son to be alone if something happened. And when something did happen, when her son was lying breathless in a field, her son wasn't alone. He was comforted by a blonde-haired, blue-eyed boy that only her son could see. A praying mom had turned her son over to God, trusting he would be there for him. And he was. A praying mom had started a prayer chain during a crisis. God answered those prayers.

~⁖~

For he will command his angels concerning you
to guard you in all your ways.

Psalm 91:11 NIV

~⁖~

Pause to Ponder

How often do you put your full trust in God? How often do you depend on his protection for yourself or another? It is sometimes difficult for us to let go of our need to worry, our need to be in control. We can't control everything, so we need to adjust our mindset. We need to turn our worries over to the Lord. It is only then that we can have sweet sleep. Because we can't control everything, we need to read the Bible and be in prayer. We need to talk to God and tell him our concerns and our worries. Finally, we need to exercise the big T. Trust! We must trust God to handle all these things we feel a need to fear and worry about. When we do hand it all over to God, we can finally experience that refreshing, sweet sleep. Why? Because we know that God is in control. We don't have to worry. Yes, we do have a choice about it.

So, how have you been sleeping lately? Is there anything you have been worrying about? Have you talked to God about it? Have you asked for his help and protection? Have you placed that heavy burden of worry on outstretched arms and handed it off to God? Once you have done that, go ahead. Sleep in. Enjoy that wonderful sweet sleep that God has promised you.

Our God is mighty. Our God is powerful. And our God gets us through so many difficult and painful things. When we are too weak to bear it, when our knees are buckling, he's holding us up. When we don't see how it can be done, we know that he can. And when we need him most, he is there for us. We are weak. He is strong.

Pause for Prayer

Oh Lord,

You are the most loving Father we could ever ask for. You listen to our concerns. You hear our prayers. When it comes to our children, we have a hard time letting go of worry. We don't want anything bad to happen to them. There is much we can find to worry about, Lord, but you have told us we don't need to worry. Help us remember to give our worries to you. Help us to trust you to care for our children and our loved ones when we feel anxious. We marvel at all that you do to protect us and our loved ones. Our hearts rejoice at the miracles you sometimes perform. Some things we are aware of, and others we are not. Use those things to remind us of your care. Use those things to draw us closer to you and trust you even more. Thank you for your loving protection. Thank you for your answers to prayer. Thank you for providing a means so that our sleep can be sweet, even in a world trying to lure us into worrying.

In Jesus's Name.
Amen.

CHAPTER 32

The Calling

Living in New Mexico and having a career there for many years left Serenity with a strong attachment. Even so, her roots in Wisconsin were calling her home. Her mother was aging. She knew it was time to go home. With 25 years in the Veterans Administration (VA), she tried to get a transfer from New Mexico to a VA close to home in Wisconsin. Where ordinarily this would have probably worked out, the timing just wasn't right. The government had a hiring freeze in place.

Serenity's mother tried to help by sending Serenity newspapers with help wanted ads. A clinic in a city nearby was advertising for visiting nurses. Serenity called them and inquired about the position. The position required in-home visits, changing bandages, doing IVs and catheters. Serenity told them she was a psych nurse. She would need a refresher course. The human resources person asked her to hold on while passing her on to another nurse who was starting an in-home psychiatric visiting nurse program. She interviewed Serenity, and she offered her the position. Serenity retired from the VA and accepted the job.

She enjoyed working the new job, but it did not pay well. Within a year, Medicare stopped paying for the service, so the position was abolished. The clinic wanted her to stay on as a home care nurse. She loved the people, so she decided to do a refresher course and accept the position. She worked in-home care, and she loved it.

Eventually, Serenity received a call asking if she would help out with a couple of hospice nurses in her area. She reluctantly agreed. They kept asking her for help week after week.

At the death of a patient, Serenity was present for her first hospice death. She was at peace. Her heart was smiling. The patient had been medicated right and his family was all on the same page and comforted with how they had handled the situation. She took care of a few more patients. After one particular death she attended, she left with such peace.

When Serenity went into the hospice patient's homes she would ask, "Jesus, be my guide and put your words in my mouth." One day, as she left a hospice visit, she went out to her car. She said, "I believe this is my calling. Father, if you want me to be a hospice nurse, I know I will be one." She turned it all over to God and awaited his answer.

The hospice nurses she was temporarily helping all told her they were going to stay until they retired as they loved their jobs. They said if there was ever an opening they would love to have her.

It appeared it was going to be a long wait for Serenity to get a position in hospice care. It appeared that way, but God had a plan. He also had a timetable.

Three days later, one of the nurses who said she would never leave put in her resignation, saying she was going to move out of state. That nurse's boyfriend had gotten a job in Minnesota, so she moved when he did. That left a vacancy in the hospice nurses—a vacancy that was filled by Serenity.

When it seemed it would be a long wait for Serenity to have an opening for that job, God had other plans. He wanted his caring nurse to minister to the dying. He made room for her, unexpectedly. He did so only after her heartfelt prayer that was said in expectation.

God had nudged Serenity with a desire to care for and minister to the terminally ill. Serenity had told God she wanted to do this important work for him. Then she put it in his hands and waited for his decision. How amazing that there was such a turn of events in only three days!

God knows what he wants each of us doing. He loves a willing servant responding to his call. Responding to his nudges. You see, when God gets involved in human resources, anything can happen.

∽

Commit to the Lord whatever you do,
and he will establish your plans.

Proverbs 16:3 NIV

∽

Pause to Ponder

God has plans and a purpose for each of us. He loves it when we respond to his calls and his nudges. We should never assume that those longings he puts in our hearts will not be fulfilled. Go to him in prayer. Talk with him like you would your best friend. Share your willingness to do his will. Step out in trust and wait to see what he will do. He can make a way when we don't see one.

Pause for Prayer

Dear Lord,

We thank you for those times you put a burning desire in our hearts to do something for you and your kingdom. Those times when you clearly nudge us and move our hearts in ways that are undoubtable. We praise you for moving mountains that stand between us and doing those tasks you would have us do. We thank you for giving us persistence and confidence to pray, trust, and believe in you for what sometimes feels impossible to us. We thank you for all the times you make things align in our lives that we could not possibly do on our own. We thank you, Lord, for taking care of us so that we can take care of others.

In Jesus's name.
Amen.

CHAPTER 33

The Master Tapissier

Even at four years old, she questioned it. Why had she grown up without a dad? The loss and resentment were overwhelming. She thought it was the worst thing that could have happened to her. She had known something was wrong since she was little. She was very intuitive.

Finally, when Carol was thirty-nine, her mother revealed the secret. It happened six weeks before Carol was born. It was also the day after her brother's first birthday. On that fateful day, her father was murdered. The circumstances surrounding the murder were horrific and were not discussed in the family. Learning of the details and the people involved was even more shocking and unnerving. Life would never be the same for her family. These events from years ago led her mom to move back to the small town where she came from to be by her family.

It was all part of God's plan. Carol was spared being married at twelve, having kids, and an early divorce like happened to most young girls where she had been born. She can see God's hand in that. If she would have stayed where she was born, she never would have gone to a Lutheran church or a Lutheran grade school, high school, and college. If she would have stayed there, she never would have become a Lutheran school teacher. Clearly, God was positioning Carol for her calling.

Carol was nudged by God to be a Lutheran school teacher. She knew this would be a special and humble walk to take in her life. She received her degree, which was followed by a call as a Lutheran elementary school teacher. What a blessing to be able to share God's Word with these precious young children on a daily basis! As she settled into teaching, she could relate to the single moms and she could relate to the kids too. After all, she had grown up raised by a single mom. She had many children in her classes from a home with a single parent.

Carol knew that God allows things to happen to us so that we can help others based on our experiences. Carol wanted to know all she could so she could better understand those disadvantaged children. She took counseling classes to help increase her understanding of what the children in her classroom were dealing with. She knew that teaching these children really involved more than just academics. She was concerned about the parents. She was also concerned about young souls and their well-being, as well.

Through the years of teaching, Carol became angry at how some of the parents were abusing and neglecting their children. Some of the parents were drug addicts. Some of the student's mothers had been abused themselves as children. Sometimes, the cycle of abuse continues from one generation to the next. Unfortunately, the children usually hid what was going on in their home life. One year, as she was teaching first grade, Carol learned of an incident that happened to one of her students. A very controlling father had killed the family's pet in front of his children. Imagine the trauma for those children!

Caring can be painful. If the children have someone who cares about them and if they get help, the children can recover, but it won't be easy. As much as she wanted to, Carol found out that she couldn't change their way of life. She recognized all she could do is love them. God had given her much love to give to those children.

Carol spent most of her teaching years working in a large city and later in a small town. Carol was a person who cares deeply. Not everyone cares as much as she did. Every school she went to, there was a problem that needed to be dealt with.

Teaching is not an easy job. Considering the emotions of teaching young, vulnerable children with a difficult home life adds to the challenges. But Carol was up for the challenge and determined to make a difference for others. With a heart full of compassion, she showed love to the students. And then, the unthinkable happened. A co-worker turned on her and got several mothers to follow her example. Carol was slandered. It was unimaginable. She was slandered by a fellow teacher in a Christian school. It was not something one would expect. She was asked to leave the school. How could this happen? She thought she was doing as God wanted her to do with her life and now this! Carol was in disbelief and devastated.

Carol had worked her entire life to be able to serve these precious little ones and the Lord. There was more disappointment and loss in her life. It was all too much. She almost had a breakdown. Satan loves such opportunities to crush our spirit. But Carol wasn't going to have it. God put caring Christian friends in her life. Friends who loved, encouraged, and supported her.

Despite the challenging and disappointing times Carol was enduring, she promised God that she would be faithful. Carol knew that Jesus understood what she was dealing with as she went through the hard times. She knew that he understood because he had been rejected, too.

Carol's promise to be faithful to God was the beginning of a career with many forks in the path. A path that Carol followed as long as she discerned she was being led by God to serve. God used her to impact many lives.

The first teaching day after she left her job was spent attending a funeral. It was the first of many. During the course of four years, twenty-four of Carol's family members and friends died. She lost her grandmother and her uncle to cancer. She lost her real mom and two wonderful ladies who looked at her as their daughter. These ladies were from the churches where she taught. She thought of one of these ladies as her adopted mom. This lady had never had any children of her own, but she adopted Carol.

Such devastating loss takes a toll. Carol joined a grief support group. Life changed once again. There was good, and there was bad. Carol learned about setting goals to help herself through the grief. She learned to give herself permission to grieve.

Carol made it through all of this change and loss by the grace of God—that undeserved love of God that Christians are so blessed with. It resulted in her growing and reaching out to others.

Carol realized that God was at work in her life. There was a tapestry of her life in the making. God was using all of these experiences to weave this tapestry. Much like living our lives, tapestry weaving seems to be a challenge, but God is the Master Tapissier.

Despite the devastation of having her calling of teaching taken away from her, Carol knew that God had other plans for her. She lives her life as a megaphone announcing the words of Jeremiah.

"For I know the plans I have for you," declares the LORD,
"plans to prosper you and not to harm you,
plans to give you hope and a future.
Then you will call on me and come and pray to me,

and I will listen to you.
You will seek me and find me
when you seek me with all your heart."

Jeremiah 29:11-13 NIV

That was Carol. She followed God's lead for the plans he had for her. She went where he led her. She found her hope and her future in him. She was always seeking and finding him. Always calling on him and praying to him. Always following where he led her.

She knew God wanted her to meet other people. She knew there was other work that God had for her to do. Carol soon went to work at a prison. She had many experiences there.

It wasn't long before several of the prison employees started noticing some things about Carol. "You're not like them," she was told. It seems her co-workers were afraid of her because she wasn't like them. Her Christianity was showing. Those glints of gold sparkling through from her tapestry were being noticed. So was her love for others and her nurturing nature. She was teaching inmates the difference between right and wrong. Teaching them responsibility and morality. Carol wasn't going to toss these people aside. She knew someone needed to care and impact the prisoners and their mindset. While there, she talked to a lady about God before her life ended. Carol knew she had gone to heaven.

Carol was an advocate for resolving prison incidents. If there was trouble, she told the prisoners to admit it when they had done something wrong. She told them to take their punishment and not do it again. She told them what her mom had always told her.

Her teaching started to have an impact on prisoners. One day after an incident, the Captain said to her, "I don't know why, but they are admitting they did it." Carol knew why. She had taught them to be honest. There was something new happening at the prison. Change was coming. Carol had triggered it thanks to a nudge from God.

The prisoners didn't seem to have any concept of punishment. There were rules to abide by and consequences for those who didn't abide by the rules. But were the prisoners aware of the consequences? Did they make the connection? After these incidents, there were hearings. In the hearings, a prisoner would be found guilty or not guilty and then be given a consequence. By recording all hearings and consequences on a spreadsheet each week, the guards were made aware of the consequences so they could make sure they were carried out. This could possibly be a dress rehearsal for life on the outside if they only began to understand the impact of disobedience versus obeying the rules.

Often, prisoners would have need of medical care. Over and over, one prisoner would be transported from the prison to Madison to see a doctor. This was an expensive proposition for the taxpayer. The charge for each trip was $500. Very often, when they arrived at the doctor's office, the prisoner would refuse to see the doctor. What was the incentive for a prisoner to go to the doctor only to refuse to see him upon arrival? It seems the prisoner knew that he would get lunch at a favorite fast food restaurant during those trips to the doctor. In time, the prison started giving the prisoners who refused to see the doctor a sack lunch instead of fast food. When the prison started charging $500 for a trip, the word spread throughout the prison, and the needless trips ceased. The goal was for the prisoners to see there were consequences to their actions and poor choices.

Some of the prisoners would take the prison towels and cut them up to be washcloths. The prison started charging them for the towels. Suddenly, the practice of cutting the towels up stopped.

Many of the prisoners had hearings. If the prisoners were not notified about their hearings, they would sue. Carol made sure they were all notified and had to sign that they were notified. Suddenly, the lawsuits stopped.

Carol felt the prisoners needed some help to be able to grasp the concept of punishment for disobedience. Carol gave the prison units a list of the punishments so that they would be informed and hopefully motivated to stop doing some of these troublesome behaviors. It was all about teaching the prisoners that there are repercussions for not following the rules. She went beyond what was required of her to try to help the prisoners rehabilitate themselves and be better prepared to care for themselves if they got released back into society.

After several years, Carol went to work for probation and parole. Sometimes, life was far too serious. Depression and anxiety took a toll on some of the probationers. One day a probationer slit his wrists outside of the office of a mental health unit. Imagine the hopelessness felt by someone to resort to such measures. Working for the Department of Corrections certainly was a lot for the employees to contend with.

Carol tried to help break some of the tension as opportunities arose. There was a singing fish on the wall of the Probation and Parole office. One day the singing fish disappeared. Carol started a story about it. This helped to break the tension. She was always working on that relationship with her co-workers. A relationship that might open the door to sharing Jesus.

Carol learned that many of the people in prison and on probation had rough beginnings in life. Their needs had not been met when they were children. She could relate to this after having been a teacher to children that had been in similar situations. Looking back, Carol feels that many of the things that had happened in her life were working together as preparation for the things to come.

Throughout her various career choices, Carol displayed one thing consistently. She cared. It is painful to care. As God led her down multiple career paths, he was weaving more of her life's tapestry.

Among her many jobs, Carol worked in a Group Home for Psychotics. This type of mental illness encompasses many variations of the ability to make sound judgments, think clearly, deal with day-to-day life, recognize reality, and behave as society would expect. The individuals in the Group Home were on many medications. One of the men had lived through a tornado. This had affected him greatly. Previously, he had been a cook. To try to bring him back to reality, Carol brought in some zucchini one day. "Would you make me some Zucchini Bread?" she asked. He complied. Eventually, he began to cook other things, as well. Carol was helping him to find a purpose.

Another place that God needed Carol's caring contributions was in an Assisted Living facility. There was a resident there that Carol affectionately named Betty Booper. The woman had dementia. Dementia is a difficult thing to deal with. Some dementia patients drift in and out of reality. One night, as Carol worked the night shift, she found that Betty was non-responsive. Carol knew Betty's departure time was drawing near. She sang "Jesus Loves Me" and prayed the Lord's Prayer. Just as the Amen rolled off Carol's lips, Betty opened her eyes, looked at Carol, and said, "Thank you." Just as quickly, she took her last breath. Betty had gone to be with the Lord. Carol had escorted her on her journey home. What a precious gift to give.

The needs of the elderly are emotionally draining, but they are such a blessing to those who care for them. One day, Carol spent four hours talking with an elderly man about God. The man was a Christian. He wanted to die. He thought that he needed to work his way to heaven. Carol knew better. She knew that the words of Ephesians were true.

❧

For it is by grace you have been saved, through faith—
and this is not from yourselves, it is the gift of God—
not by works, so that no one can boast.

Ephesians 2:8-9 NIV

❧

Carol helped him to see that God had already ensured that he qualified for heaven. She knew this man needed that gift of God. Carol knew that we couldn't make our tapestry by ourselves. Yet, even after talking to and reassuring him that he was forgiven, he still felt he had to earn his way to heaven. He is still alive, not willing to let go because he felt he had not done enough to earn his way into heaven.

Despite all of the work-related nudges from God, Carol had other nudges from God. Every day for twenty-two years, Carol prayed for a child of her own. She thought of being a foster parent, but she hadn't acted on it. Many years later, God answered her prayers.

A girl was about to come into Carol's life. Carol worked with the husband of the girl's teacher. The parents had dumped her things in a garbage bag and dropped her off at the Salvation Army. How could a parent do this to their child? The young girl had mental issues and was short in stature. She was missing part of her arm. The diabetic nineteen-year-old girl was a special education student. In the past, the girl had attempted suicide twice. They brought her to meet Carol and she moved in with Carol.

During this time, there were many instances of religious discussion between the girl and Carol. Much time was spent talking about the girl's life. She finally admitted that cutting no longer made her feel better. Carol got her counseling, glasses, and hearing aids. The summer that she graduated from high school, Carol had a party for her. Her parents came to the party. After seven months of living with Carol, the girl decided she wanted to have her own place. She moved out. Carol kept in touch with her for years after graduation. Then, one summer, Carol and the girl's parents attended her wedding. The girl who was an answer to prayer. A girl for Carol to love. A girl who had needed Carol.

As the years went by, Carol faced some physical challenges as well. She had a knee replacement, weight loss surgery, a broken hip, a hip replacement, and eventually, her other knee replaced. There was pain and an interruption to her daily life. There was also an interruption to her income and additional expenses. There was a ten-and-one-half-week stay in a nursing home for rehabilitation. There were one-and-one-half years of not being able to physically do what she used to do. Carol needed to go back to work. She went to work for an agency that needed caregivers to go into the homes of patients and help them at certain hours of the day. She continues to do this important work.

"Life is like a tapestry," Carol says. "It looks good on the front side, but turn it over and see all the loose ends. God is at work on those."

Carol feels we all have a choice in how we lead our lives. She wants a computer printout of God's plans. God gives us freedom of choice. Sometimes, it is hard to know what the decision should be. She asks God to please bless whatever decision she makes.

If you see a lady wearing a beautiful sweatshirt…a sweatshirt that resembles a tapestry…a tapestry with strands of gold shining brightly, it just might be Carol. She shines brightly for others to see. She's always adding to that tapestry with the help of God.

When she looks back, Carol can see God's hand in her life. She may not understand all that has happened in her life, but she understands a great deal of it. What about the parts she doesn't understand? It's okay. Carol knows it is all part of God's plan for her. She trusts his plans are not to harm her but to give her hope and a future. Why? Because he said so. Because he nudged her. Because she is nudged to serve God wherever he places her.

For now, she is happy to work in her apprenticeship under the Master Tapissier. Striving to be always faithful. Always aware that God is working on all those loose threads until the tapestry is finished. Trusting that God will be pleased with the finished tapestry as long as she continues to follow him.

⁓

But he knows the way that I take;
When he has tested me, I will come forth as gold.

Job 23:10 NIV

⁓

Pause to Ponder

Finding our place in the world is a big deal. For some people, it takes their entire life. Others know right away what they are called to do. For most, it is ever-evolving. We all have a role to play, a mission. It is given to us by God. God is the Tapissier of our life. He is the Master Weaver. We are his apprentice training under him. He leads us, and we humbly follow.

You may have one goal in mind. God may have another. Have you found your purpose? If not, ask him today to reveal it to you. As he leads you to fulfill his purpose in you, pray for guidance and use discernment. You may want to do one thing. God may lead you to do another. He might nudge you, move you. It is all part of the process of weaving our tapestry of life. We know how we want the top side to look, but God does his best work on the underside—most times out of view. Do you see all those loose threads? He has a plan for those. He will bring it all together. When he is done, turn the cloth over and look. Look at the beautiful tapestry of your life. Did you follow his lead so that the finished side on the top looks the way he wants it to look?

We look at all the loose threads on the underside of our tapestry with disappointment. We see the disorganized pattern, the incomplete areas, the jagged threads, and feel disheartened. God looks at the finished side of our tapestry. He can see the glints of gold within the threads of our tapestry as the light of his spirit reflects off of them to others.

Pause for Prayer

Dear Lord,

We have many plans for life, but you are the one in control. Help us to remember that. Help us to recognize that where you lead us, we must follow. Give us encouragement when our plans don't work out the way we had hoped. Lift us up and give us new purpose. Remind us of your love and concern for us. Give us the right attitude as we face life's many challenges. Give us the strength and the courage to follow your lead. Help us to make a difference wherever you place us. Thank you for your nudges, Lord. Use us for your higher purpose.

In Jesus's name.
Amen.

CHAPTER 34

Blanket of Peace

Martha was raised a churchgoer. After marriage, she and her husband, Tyler, attended church together. Even though she was a believer, there was a puzzle piece missing from her life.

One day, following church services, Martha and Tyler came out of church assessing the situation. They felt like they were just going through the motions. They needed to grow their faith. They needed a relationship with the Lord. They needed the knowledge and hope contained in God's Word found in the Bible, but they weren't even being offered Bible classes. There was a painful realization that their faith was stagnant. With that revelation, they left their lifelong denomination of faith behind while seeking a church that would fill that void.

God had a plan. He saw a couple that was seeking. Seeking him. Seeking his Word. God wasn't going to let them down. He was going to nudge them. He was about to use someone to lead them to the Word and create a real relationship with God. As always, God's timing was impeccable.

And we know that in all things
God works for the good of those who love him,
who have been called according to his purpose.

Romans 8:28 NIV

Soon, God set his plan in motion. One of Tyler's clients invited them to her house for a Bible study. Tyler encouraged Martha to go, but she was reluctant. She felt threatened. Although she had been a lifelong member of the church, she didn't know anything about the Bible. Eventually, she agreed to go, but she went there with a defensive attitude. Very quickly, she recognized that this Bible study was much more important than she imagined. It changed her life.

The leader of the Bible study was a woman. She was on fire for the Lord. She loved sharing the Word and she couldn't get enough of the Word. At 54 years old, she went back to school to get a theology degree. She didn't become a minister. She just wanted the biblical knowledge and liked to bring people to God.

By the time Martha and Tyler left that first class, Martha thought it all made so much sense. Martha knew this was something she needed to gain more knowledge. She felt a strong urge to encapsulate to learn more. It felt so right. God was moving her!

The woman leading the Bible study had such a presence to her. It was like the Holy Spirit was at work in her. She was like an angel that came into Martha's life just when she needed her. Tyler felt the same.

This was all very new to Martha. Previously, she never understood the Bible. She never looked at it. Before, she didn't feel like she had a relationship with the Lord. She was going through a ritualistic religion. But now, she was being exposed to the Word of God through the Bible study. Her eyes and her heart had been opened. Soon Martha was going to be glad to have this new relationship to draw on.

Just six months later, Martha would draw on her newly strengthened faith as never before. Martha was about to face a frightening diagnosis. She had an MRI and was told she had a spinal tumor. This tumor was located in the cauda equina. Its name is derived from Latin and means horse's tail. It is the part of your body that is at the end of your spinal cord. It contained all the nerves that make your body function from the waist down. Martha's tumor was inside of all those nerves.

This was a very serious condition, and the doctors didn't know if they could remove it. If they were unable to remove the tumor, Martha would eventually become paralyzed from the waist down as the tumor increased in size. The doctors determined they needed to perform surgery with the hope that they could remove the tumor.

The situation was very frightening to Martha. She was going to have surgery, not knowing what she was going to wake up to. The doctors wouldn't know until they performed the surgery if, in trying to get the tumor out, they may have to destroy various nerves. Damage to these nerves could cause foot drop. Foot drop affects your gait. It is when you walk, and your foot just drops. You drag your toes along the ground or bend the knees lifting the foot higher than normal so that you avoid dragging the toes.

Damage to these nerves could also cause loss of bladder or bowel control. It could also impact this young mother's reproduction capabilities.

The Bible study that brought Martha's faith to maturity was six months prior to her tumor diagnosis. She was a baby Christian. She felt like her faith was being tested when she was diagnosed. She felt very fearful. She felt threatened.

More than fearing a malignant tumor, she dealt with the fear of not being able to remove the tumor because of the ramifications. She could be paralyzed from the waist down. What if important nerves had to be severed?

Martha decided there was only one thing that she could do. She put all her trust in the Lord. She loved the picture of Proverbs 3:5-6.

❦

Trust in the LORD with all your heart
and lean not on your own understanding;
in all your ways submit to him,
and he will make your paths straight.

Proverbs 3:5-6 NIV

❦

It was a testimony of her faith at that time. She didn't know where to put all her fear. She decided to turn it all over to the Lord and let him carry her through the storm. She totally surrendered herself to the Lord and let his will be done.

The day of the surgery came, and with it the apprehension and concerns. It was all in God's hands. Fortunately, God guided the surgeon's hands, and the doctors were able to remove the tumor. The only nerve they destroyed was to her big toe. As a result, her big toe is numb. Otherwise, the six-hour surgery was successful.

Two days after her surgery, the doctors had shocking news. They wanted Martha to have a CAT scan of her brain. They thought the tumor originated in her brain, dislodged, and traveled through her spinal fluid, ending up in her lower lumbar, where the tumor continued to grow. This was very rare. She had to have MRIs for the next five years to make sure she didn't have any more brain tumor activity. This is a long time to have that hanging over you. It proved to be quite a trial.

Martha had some wonderful people in her life at that time. She found comfort in her faith to go through that surgery when she turned to God. He gave her a blanket of comfort…a blanket of peace. That blanket helped ease the fear of the uncertainty. She couldn't find that kind of comfort anywhere else. It underscored that we have God through the bad times and the good times. Going through this life-changing event as a 34-year-old mother of a toddler certainly caused some fear.

Through it all, what amazed Martha is the love of the Lord. He gave her the added strength, perseverance, and confidence to get her through it. He blessed her with his faithfulness.

If she hadn't been to that Bible study, just six months prior, how different things would have been. Without the assurance of God's protection, she would have been depressed and lost. How would she have gotten through it? Martha clearly recognized that being on our own is not enough.

This encounter gave her the foundation to know that we can lean on God and trust him. She has relied on that faith and trust ever since those days.

When tragedies happen, some people blame God. Rather, Martha thanks God for the faith she has. She believes God helps us handle what we are given.

God has proven to her time and again that though she may have to go through these trials, he is with her in the end on the other side. These things can be frightening and overwhelming. They may drop you to your knees, but just knowing that God is with you through those things gives you peace. Through that peace, we don't have to understand everything on our own.

It's been over thirty years since Martha and Tyler went to that first Bible study, and they have never looked back. They joined an Evangelical Church. They continue to go to Bible study. They feel it helps to be on the same level of belief and knowledge. During that time, Martha has had many other difficulties. She finds the difficulties strengthen her faith. She is thankful she has that foundation to draw on. A foundation she received from someone eager to share God's Word with others. Someone on fire for the Lord.

Too often, when bad things happen to people, they ask God, "Why?" Martha has the attitude of "Why not?" We are going to know pain and grief. We are going to suffer and have trials. These are trials of this earth. It is challenging when these things happen.

Martha knows that this earth is not our permanent home. She takes comfort in knowing that we have something better to look forward to and that it is going to be eternal. How does she know? God's Word tells her so.

God's Word provides Martha that blanket of peace...all shook out, fluffed up, and softly falling to envelope her with daily reminders of God's loving care.

⤦

You will keep in perfect peace those whose minds are steadfast, because they trust in you.

Isaiah 26:3 NIV

⤦

Pause to Ponder

Like so many others, Martha was on a journey. Each person's journey is unique. Martha was always a believer. So why did she feel so empty? Why did she have this yearning for something more, something better? When you haven't heard of or experienced anything different, you don't know what you are missing. But Martha was sure there was something missing.

Sometimes, God sends us a person. Someone who can point us in the right direction. Someone who can make the Bible come alive for us. Someone who is on fire for Jesus. Martha found that person for her. That person helped Martha see the way. That person helped Martha see what she had been missing, even though she was a believer. That changed everything for Martha.

It can be a little scary to change up our ways from what has been taught to us our entire lives. We can be hesitant when learning about different ways. Which way is the right way? Is this the way I should go? It can take quite an adjustment to make changes to our comfortable routine. It can take prayer and discernment. Martha was growing in her faith. It was a blessing. God's perfect timing of all these changes in her life helped Martha prepare for the challenges she would face in the future.

What was Martha's mathematical equation to find what was missing in her life? An on-fire friend, plus fearless faith, plus ferocious trust. The sum of those equals peace. God's heavenly peace. That peace provided the confidence she needed to get in the right mindset when dealing with her rare illness.

Pause for Prayer

Dear Lord,

When we learn to listen to that still small voice in our hearts, we grow closer to you. Thank you for that blessing. When we take the action that you nudge us towards, we are serving you, growing our faith, and working towards a life that is pleasing to you. We sometimes don't know what we need, Lord. You do. In your omniscience, you always know. You lead us. You nudge us. Help us to be sensitive to your nudges, Lord. Help us to respond as you would have us respond. Please make your nudges clear to us. Give us the strength and courage to be on fire for you. Please lead your people to start a wildfire for the Lord. A wildfire that spreads rapidly in people's hearts. A wildfire of faith burning with the desire to praise and serve you, Almighty God. As they do so, Lord, bless your people with your blanket of peace.

In Jesus's precious name.
Amen.

CHAPTER 35

Free from Bondage

She called herself a Christian. She even taught Sunday school. She prayed about it. She wanted to quit, but she always picked the bottle back up.

By sixth grade, Mariah had her first beer. By age thirteen, she wanted to quit drinking and quit smoking pot. Her friends could easily quit whenever they wanted, but Mariah couldn't. She got headaches. Her drinking was different than most.

The struggles of alcoholism are real and powerful. There is much guilt and shame. For the next twenty-nine years, she quit drinking many times. Mariah would switch addictions. She would quit drinking and start eating. Eating too much. She tried to quit drinking on her own. She had also gone through some professional programs to try to quit drinking. With a bachelor's degree in health and wellness, Mariah knew what to do, but she couldn't do it. At least not by herself.

Then, after many years, things got real, and God touched Mariah in a way like never before. At forty-two, she got her second drunk driving ticket. She had her children in the car. Facing a felony, she knew she would lose everything…her children, her home, her career. Imagine the devastation and humiliation this must have caused. Think of the turmoil and conflict her life must have been in. It all must have felt completely out of control and very frightening.

God had not abandoned Mariah. He nudged her to make some changes. She decided to do whatever it took to break the cycle. Mariah went to counseling and entered an outpatient rehabilitation program. She started working through the steps of Alcoholics Anonymous (AA). Step One involved Mariah admitting she had an alcohol problem and that she was unable to stop drinking on her own. Mariah had done that.

Step Two involved Mariah recognizing that a power greater than herself would help restore her to sanity. That power, for Mariah, was God.

Mariah had worked her way to Step Six, which consisted of admitting all of her character defects to another person. After twenty-nine years of drinking, Mariah had to confess all that she had done wrong because of her drinking. This was a lot to face. Many of those things were very embarrassing. Mariah thought back to her youth when she went to Sunday school. She had become a person that little girl in Sunday school never dreamed she would be. God was working on her heart and opening her eyes.

Mariah had a sincere heart. She wanted a better life. She wanted to quit drinking. During this time, she was taking an Antabuse pill. It is a medication used for treating alcohol use disorders. These pills make you get sick if you drink. It was a useful tool to help Mariah quit drinking. On the morning of March 17th, 2004, she looked at that pill and thought, "This is the only thing keeping me from drinking?"

The guilt and shame had kept her sick. She was ready to be well again. Looking at that pill, she said, "If this is the only thing helping me to quit drinking, this little pill is my god." Mariah got down on her knees and cried out, "Jesus, I knew you as a little girl, but I don't even know you anymore. I do know you're not this little white pill. Please, make yourself real to me." With that sincere prayer for God's mercy and grace, she begged for his help. Life was about to change for Mariah. God had heard her heartfelt cries.

Later that night, she went to bed. In the middle of the night, she heard her name being called. Mariah, Mariah. When she woke up, she couldn't understand. She wondered why her children were calling her by her first name in the middle of the night. She decided to check on them. She was on her way to her children's room, but she only made it to the living room. She was brought to her knees. Filled with overwhelming emotion, Mariah had increased awareness and could see all the damage the alcoholism had done in her life. She saw how it was destroying the lives of her family. She could see the magnitude of her alcoholism. In that moment, as she was on her knees and reflecting on her situation, God nudged her. He moved her to make some changes. She ached to be a part of the solution and not the problem.

Mariah felt the Lord put it on her heart that he had made her beautiful again. That she was no longer that broken, alcoholic woman. That she was forgiven, made new, and his treasure as white as snow. As beautiful as a virgin again. The old was gone, and the new was here, and she was not that old person. She realized that he could do anything and that nothing was too much for God. In her bathroom, there were some beautiful pink sheets. She doesn't remember buying them, yet there they were. She put them on her bed and made a new commitment to the Lord to honor him in her body.

In the excitement of the change God had made in her, Mariah called her aunt in the middle of the night. She said, "Cora, I got a gift." "What kind of gift?" asked Cora. "It's a gift from God," said Mariah. "I am not ashamed anymore. I am not that person anymore, so I can talk about what I did." Mariah knew that she was a new creation in Christ.

Therefore, if anyone is in Christ, the new creation has come:
The old has gone, the new is here!

2 Cor 5:17 NIV

Mariah was gaining insight from the Bible. She knew she was Christ's treasured possession.

For you are a people holy to the LORD your God.
Out of all the peoples on the face of the earth,
the LORD has chosen you to be his treasured possession.

Deuteronomy 14:2 NIV

At that moment, she didn't think she'd ever sin again, but of course, we all do. When she sins, when she is down on herself, she has to remember who she is in Jesus. She reminds herself that he takes her sin and gives her his goodness. Mariah knows that she is beautiful because Christ is in her, not because of what she's done.

Mariah had been living most of her life in bondage. She was a slave to the bottle. She was imprisoned by a very powerful addiction. Some people never conquer that addiction. Fortunately, Mariah was able to break out of her addiction prison. She had found her freedom. She found it in Jesus and with the help of Alcoholics Anonymous (AA). Jesus said that everyone who sins is a slave to sin. Mariah had been a slave to the bottle. She knew that freedom could be available to her. She clung to Jesus's words found in John 8:36 NIV, "*So if the Son sets you free, you will be free indeed.*" Mariah longed to be free. She knew that Jesus could set her free in every way.

Addiction had affected every part of Mariah's life. Before, she was afraid. She was embarrassed about who she had been. Now, she could talk about how Christ set her free. Before, she was riddled with guilt and shame. Now, he took away that guilt and shame. She was made new through what Jesus did on the cross. It was amazing to think what he had done for her and that she was made new.

Mariah had a strong weapon that helped her in the fight to become free and remain free. That weapon was the Word of God found in the Bible. It was filled with reminders and hope. She didn't want to forget that she was a treasured possession. During the last nineteen years of her life, she has spent much time reflecting. She gets strength from Matthew 6:33 NIV. *But seek first his kingdom and his righteousness, and all these things will be given to you as well.*

Mariah already knew many of these things, but the bondage she was in had kept her from her freedom. Mariah didn't want to forget. She made a dedication to seek Christ first, read the Bible, listen to the Holy Spirit, put a priority on her family, and seek companionship with other Christians. She knew that she needed to remember that Jesus died so she could be forgiven. No matter what—she must never forget.

Mariah's walk with God is very important to her. She still gets down on herself because she knows she is still a sinner. She reminds herself to read the Bible, be diligent in her prayers, vigilant in her lifestyle, and always remember she is his treasured possession.

Looking back, Mariah realizes that the guilt and shame kept her sick through her days of alcoholism. She thinks often about the great exchange—how Jesus came and exchanged his life for ours. She remembers this happened all because of God's love for us. He gives us eternal life. She tries to focus on the simplicity of the gospel. Through it all, Mariah has come to a realization. Her life is just better with Christ in it. With that realization, she was nudged to leave her life of bondage.

As we strive to overcome life's challenges, God provides many tools to help us. Alcoholics Anonymous (AA) and behavioral health counseling were critical in Mariah's early recovery. Mariah still attends AA meetings and continues to find good fellowship there. For her long-term recovery, these tools are still important, but her relationship with Jesus is the most important piece of how she stays clean. Her recovery is now based on a continual surrender to Jesus. It's a surrender of the sins that plague her.

Ever since the Lord became part of Mariah's recovery, she has maintained long-term sobriety. It's been nineteen years since the Lord touched her that day. She's been clean ever since. Prior to that, while using secular treatment programs alone, the most she had been able to string together was ninety-nine consecutive days of sobriety. What an amazing difference the Lord can make in one's life!

Mariah still has an addiction. This is one addiction she is not going to fight against. You see, Mariah is addicted to Jesus. Yes, she traded her bottle for Jesus. In the process, she changed and saved her life. She let Jesus rescue her. He threw off those chains of bondage and set her free. Free indeed.

⤬

So if the Son sets you free, you will be free indeed.

John 8:36 NIV

⤬

Pause to Ponder

Life can be heavy. Challenges can take over and weigh us down. Suddenly, it's more than we can handle. It can be difficult at times to see the problem. We don't want to change. Later, when we do want to change, we can't. It's just too hard. It's too overwhelming. We don't have the tools or the willpower. Recognizing the problem is an important step, but then what? How do we fix it? Are we even capable of fixing it? That's when we must surrender. Falling on our knees and calling out to God. Falling on our knees, much like Mariah did. Then trusting, praying, and waiting.

We long to be free from sin. As humans, we can't do this on our own. We need Jesus. We need repentance. But then, what joy! What an occasion to celebrate as Jesus lets us take a victory lap in our new found freedom. The freedom found through forgiveness.

Pause for Prayer

Dear Lord,

We ask your protection from those temptations that draw us in. Help us to say no. We thank you for all the times you have kept us safe from these things and the evil influences out in the world. When we are tempted and fall short, we often speak discouraging words to ourselves. Keep us in your Word so that we can encourage ourselves with your Holy Scriptures. Remind us of your love and concern for us. Encourage us with your plans for us. Lift us up with the good news of all that Jesus overcame for us. Give us a proper mindset to help us overcome our challenges. Draw us closer to you. Nudge us to be in prayer and in your Word. Strengthen us and keep us free from the bondage of sin.

We ask these things in Jesus's precious name.
Amen.

WHAT WILL YOU DO WITH YOUR NUDGES?

Life is a learning lab. We are continuously experimenting, failing, trying again and again, and eventually learning. Sometimes, God needs to send us back to be retrained. Among God's teaching tools in this learning lab are nudges. Nudges from God teach us, shape us, and give us hope and comfort to get us through those difficult times. Nudges from God's Word, from a sermon, from a time of grief, and from a failed marriage. Nudges from moments of joy and gratitude, times of need, and times of fear. Nudges from unexplained happenings. Nudges from illness and nudges from moments of sheer desperation. Nudges from abusive situations. Nudges from a faith-filled friend or a beloved family member. Nudges from strangers. Even nudges from nature. He uses them all.

My prayer for you is that you would know God better. That you would open yourself to a closer walk and deeper relationship with him and in doing so, that you are more aware of his presence in your life. My prayer for you is that you would be more attuned, more alert, and more responsive to the cues or prompts that he gives you. In other words, that you would be more aware of his nudges. He makes himself present and involved in your life far more than he is often given credit for. I pray for your awareness and recognition of his interaction and interventions in your life. I pray that you will indeed be moved by God. I pray that you will recognize and acknowledge when you have been nudged. I pray that you will be bold and tell others about what he has done for you.

❧

Let the redeemed of the LORD tell their story—
those he redeemed from the hand of the foe.

Psalm 107:2 NIV

❧

That, my friend, is a true treasure. I couldn't express my prayer for you any better than the prayer the apostle Paul wrote in Ephesians:

❧

I keep asking that the God of our Lord Jesus Christ,
the glorious Father, may give you
the Spirit of wisdom and revelation,
so that you may know him better.
I pray that the eyes of your heart
may be enlightened in order that you may know
the hope to which he has called you,
the riches of his glorious inheritance in his holy people,
and his incomparably great power for us who believe...

Ephesians 1:17-19 NIV

❧

You see, nudges take us beyond just believing in God. Nudges help us to trust and follow God. God's nudges help us build that relationship. He meets us where we are in that relationship. And then God shapes and changes our will. We receive rather than achieve these changes. We can't see faith. We can't see it grow. The gospel works quietly—as a whisper.

Be still and know that he is God. Be still and be nudged. Be nudged to change your lifestyle. Be nudged to serve others. Be nudged to forgive. To activate the power of prayer. To help lead someone to Christ. To praise him in all his glory. Be nudged to build a real relationship with God. Be nudged and be humbled. Give thanks. Be in the Word. Be nudged and put your trust in him. Be nudged to do what he would have you do. He loves you so much!

Be nudged to enlighten the eyes of your heart. Go ahead, be nudged, and know him better.

APPENDIX

Perhaps this is all new to you. Perhaps you haven't been a practicing Christian for many years. Perhaps God is being revealed to you for the first time. If that is the case and your faith is just being stirred, we'd like to provide a few extra things for you.

First of all, don't be overwhelmed! There are people in every church body willing to help you learn about God. Find a Bible-believing church that stays true to the Word of God. Start attending services. Attend Bible classes. They will be a blessing to you and help grow your faith. Don't be afraid to ask questions when you don't understand something. Study the Bible at home, as well. Why study the Bible? It is the inspired Word of God. It tells us Bible history, the good news of Jesus Christ, how to live our life, and what to expect in the future. You will be amazed at all the life situations addressed within the pages of the Bible. Don't own a Bible? There are free versions available online. Simply search for "free online Bible". There are many versions. We recommend starting with the New International Version (NIV).

PRAYER

Prayer is an important part of building a relationship with God. What is prayer anyway? Prayer is simply speaking to God from the heart. Tell him whatever is on your mind. Tell God how you feel. Tell him what your needs are. Tell him what is troubling you. Share with him your greatest challenges in life. Not sure of your purpose in life? Ask him to lead you to discover your purpose. Do you struggle with addictions, bad behaviors, or unhealthy habits? Do you have relationship problems? Yes, he can help you with that too. Just ask him. Tell him you are sorry for your wrong-doing; that is your sin. He will forgive you. Are you struggling with decisions you need to make? Need help picking a church to attend? Ask for wisdom and his guidance. Just talk to him. He is there. He listens, and he hears you. As found in 1 Peter 5:7, the New International Version of the Bible, (NIV), "Cast all your anxiety on him because he cares for you." Don't forget to thank him for all that he has done for you.

Among the eight billion people on this earth, God knows YOU! He cares for YOU! He loves YOU! Knowing that, you can go to church. Read the Bible. Join a Bible class. Pray, that is, talk to him…and believe.

Do You Need a Little Help in Your Prayers?

Start with this and just fill in the blanks.

Prayer Template

Dear Heavenly Father,

Thanks be to you for _____.

I come to you asking for your heavenly intervention to help others. If it be your will, please help _____ with _____.

I am a sinner, Lord. I have done things I shouldn't have. Please forgive my sins. Please forgive me for these sins which I have recently committed: _____, _____, and _____.

You know my weaknesses, Lord. Please strengthen me in my weakness.

Please help me with _____.

Please guide me through these challenges: _____ and _____.

Help me to learn more about you by reading and studying your Word found in the Bible. Help me learn to speak to you through prayer. Increase my faith and guide me each day.

In Jesus's name.
Amen.

The Lord's Prayer

Jesus taught this prayer, which is considered to be an example of how to pray. The Lord's Prayer is used in nearly all denominations of Christianity.

"This, then, is how you should pray: "'Our Father in heaven, hallowed be your name, your kingdom come, your will be done, on earth as it is in heaven. Give us today our daily bread. And forgive us our debts, as we also have forgiven our debtors. And lead us not into temptation, but deliver us from the evil one." **Matthew 6:9-13 NIV**

Prayer for a New Christian

Dear Father in heaven,

Thank you for revealing your Word to me. I pray that you will lead me to know the truth and increase my knowledge of you. Please come into my heart. Please forgive me my sins. Thank you for sending your son, Jesus Christ, to die for me for the forgiveness of my sins. Please lead me to a church body that delivers your true word. Give me strength to walk through life as a Christian.

In Jesus's name.
Amen.

Prayer to Recognize Our Nudges

Dear Heavenly Father,

Thanks be to you for all the blessings you give to us. We thank you for sending Jesus to die for our sins.

We live in busy and challenging times. Stress and temptation are all around us. We are faced with many decisions every day. As we spend our days on this busy and chaotic earth, we look forward to peaceful, joyful, heavenly surroundings.

We ask you to make us more aware of your presence in our lives. We humbly ask your forgiveness for losing our focus on you at times because of all the worldly distractions. Help us to discipline ourselves to find time for you each day. Help us to spend time in prayer each day. Lead us to crave and study your Word in the Bible.

As we grow in our faith in you, help us to recognize your nudges. Help us to discern your gentle calls to our hearts. Once we recognize your nudges, help us respond as you would have us respond. In this way, may we grow closer to you. May this help us to serve you and one another. Take away our fears, concerns, and stress. Put our minds in a place of peace and contentment trusting that you will help us to handle all that comes our way. Most of all, help us to know you better.

In Jesus's name.
Amen.

ACKNOWLEDGEMENTS

With gratitude to Moms in Prayer International (www.MomsInPrayer. org) and with prayers for continued blessings on your most worthy calling.

Special thanks to Pastor Steve for your expertise and valuable feedback and suggestions. You are a blessing!

Sincere thanks to those special friends and relatives who offered encouragement to me during this journey. It meant so much and you are appreciated!

Most importantly, heartfelt thanks to all those who willingly shared their God stories for this book. You did not know it at the time, but coming forward with your story was an answer to prayer. Thank you for pouring out your hearts and reliving the sometimes painful past. Thank you for sharing deeply personal and intimate events so that others may learn more about having a relationship with God. Thank you for sharing your grief, your victories, and your revelations. Thank you for sharing your everyday nudges as well as the amazing experiences in which God moved you and made you feel special. Without your candor, this book would not have been possible.

ABOUT THE AUTHOR

Susan Brownell is a heart-centered writer. She seeks to encourage readers with uplifting stories. Stories that serve a purpose. Stories that inspire. She sees stories all around her in the lives of those whose paths she crosses.

When she is not writing, Susan loves spending time with family and friends, good books and flowers. Furry friends and lively tea parties make her smile. Living in the beautiful Midwest with her husband of 56 years, she basks in the awesomeness of nature whenever she can.

Susan knows how life-changing God's nudges can be. She hopes that all of her readers experience and respond to their own personal nudges from God. And when they do, she would love to hear from them!

WOULD YOU LIKE TO HELP OTHER READERS?

Consider Leaving a Book Review Online.

It will only take a couple of minutes and it will help other readers know if they might like to read this book.

You can leave reviews for this book at Amazon.com

In the **SEARCH AMAZON Box** at the top of the page, type "**Nudged: Moved by God**"

Click on the magnifying glass.

Scroll until you see the book, then click on it.

Scroll down the page to the **Customer Reviews**.

Below the row of orange stars, look for "**Review this product**."

Click on the "**Write a customer review**" button.

If you are not yet logged in to Amazon, it will require you to login now.

You will see **"Create Review"**.

Click to indicate the number of stars you rate the book. See examples:

- To give a book a five-star review (the highest rating), click on the star at the furthest right. This means you liked the book very much.

- To give a book a three-star review (a medium rating), click on the middle star. This means you think the book is average.

- To give a book a one-star review (the lowest rating), click on the star at the furthest left. This means you did not like the book.

Add a headline (Fill this out. This is the title of your review and perhaps your main point.)

Scroll down until you see **"Add a written review."**

Type your comments about the book and click the yellow **SUBMIT** button.

Readers like it when you tell specifically what you liked about a book.

NOTE: *Even if you purchased the book elsewhere, you can still leave a review on Amazon.*

Thank you so much for helping other readers!

Would You Like a Free Gift?

Visit SusanBrownell.com and sign up!
Sure to encourage you, this free gift is a hug from me to you!

Would You Like to Read Susan's Latest Stories?

Visit SusanBrownell.com/blog

Would You Like to Know When Susan Releases More Books?

Visit SusanBrownell.com and sign up.

Do You Have a Story That Would Encourage Other Christians?

Do you have a true faith-based story that might strengthen someone's faith or help bring someone to Christ? Has God nudged you in a way that others could benefit from hearing about it? God wants us to share our experiences with others.

❧

I will give thanks to you, LORD, with all my heart;
I will tell of all your wonderful deeds.

Psalm 9:1 NIV

❧

If you have a true story that you would like to have considered to be shared in a future book, please send a few sentences about your God experience to stories@susanbrownell.com. Please include your name, email address, and phone number. If we think your story is a possible fit for a book, we will follow up with you. Stories that are accepted will have names changed to protect people's privacy.

Did this book help you?

Did it have an impact on your faith? If so, I'd love to hear from you. Please send me a message at info@SusanBrownell.com .

Thanks for reading and all of God's richest blessings to you!

Other Books by Susan Brownell

Cocoon of Love for Cancer Caregivers: Get Through the Tough Times
Cocoon of Love for Caregivers
Watch for Book 2 of the Nudged Series

www.ingramcontent.com/pod-product-compliance
Lightning Source LLC
Chambersburg PA
CBHW071408090426
42737CB00011B/1390